SCANDINAVIAN CLASSICS

Over 100 Traditional Recipes

I would like to dedicate this book to my wife who always takes care of my absentmindedness, and to my son who gives me joy on the days that feel heavy. Everything I do, I do for you.

Niklas

Skyhorse Publishing books may be purchased in bulk at special discounts for sales promotion, corporate gifts, fund-raising, or educational purposes. Special editions can also be created to specifications. For details, contact the Special Sales Department, Skyhorse Publishing, 307 West 36th Street, 11th Floor, New York, NY 10018 or info@skyhorsepublishing.com.

Skyhorse® and Skyhorse Publishing® are registered trademarks of Skyhorse Publishing, Inc.®, a Delaware corporation.

Visit our website at www.skyhorsepublishing.com

10 9 8 7 6 5 4 3 2 1

Library of Congress Cataloging-in-Publication Data is available on file.

ISBN: 978-1-62087-095-2

Printed in China

SCANDINAVIAN CLASSICS

Over 100 Traditional Recipes

Niklas Ekstedt

PHOTOGRAPHY BY HELÉN PE

TRANSLATED BY LENA GOLDEN

Skyhorse Publishing

Contents

I want to preserve our Swedish food culture.

I have not always loved classic home-style cooking. For a long time I thought that that type of food belonged to the past. I preferred to experiment with extremely difficult set-ups and to involve as much chemistry as possible—the more the difficult, the better. But today, I think differently. I want to protect our Swedish food culture, not only by passing on recipes to the next generation, but also from a financially-sustainable standpoint. It simply has to be profitable for Swedish farmers to grow the foods we have cultivated here for ages. I fear that, otherwise, we will drown in a sea of sweet chili sauce, pine nuts, and liquid smoke.

A great way to get inspired is to flip through old cookbooks, perhaps written during the last century, by writers who knew how to cook real food, from real ingredients. It is fascinating to browse through these books. They are first and foremost very beautiful, and they are filled with lots of knowledge. My favorite book from this period is Hagdahl's Cooking as Science and Art, which was originally regarded more as a work of fiction than as a cookbook Of course, you can still read it as that today, as merely entertainment. But I choose to read the recipes, make some changes, and then cook something truly delicious.

~~~

Industrialization and Cookbooks

Thanks to industrialization, Swedes were financially better off by the late 1800s. But although lthough the working and middle classes were beginning to have more money in their wallets, they lacked an upper-class education, and all the knowledge that came with it. In order to fit into better social circles, this new middle class needed to know dinner party etiquette and which foods to serve together.

This brought on a great demand for cookbooks. In addition to recipes, these included illustrated descriptions on how to fold a napkin properly and how a piece of meat should both look and smell when purchased. The demand for cookbooks grew rapidly, and by the end of the century book printers were working at full force. Never before had so many cookbooks been sold—and one of the best sellers was Charles Emil Hagdahl's book, *Cooking as Science and Art*.

The author, Charles Emil Hagdahl, was a physician, and had never had any aspirations to write a cookbook. *Cooking as Science and Art* was a result of a dinner party at the home of Hagdahl's relatives, the Abelins, in Stockholm. Hagdahl himself spoke of the incident in an interview for the magazine *Idun* in 1895. He sat at the dinner table watching the housekeeper frantically search among her papers in a chiffonier. Hagdahl asked what the housekeeper was looking for, and she replied that she was looking for a pudding recipe for dessert. Hagdahl complained that women could not keep track of their papers and spoke the words that would later be crucial for his cookbook creation:

"It really was necessary for a real man to take charge of all these scattered treasures that exist in women's family recipes and notes, and arrange them for perpetuity into something complete and manageable."

The housekeeper took this to heart and told her friends about it. A few weeks later, the doorbell rang at Hagdahl's home on the *Hötorget* square in the centre of Stockholm. Outside the door stood servants from Stockholm's most affluent families, who stood in line to hand over their families' recipes in bundles of paper. Along with the king's chef Malmgren and his niece Henrietta, Hagdahl began working on the cookbook, which would become one of the largest and most significant in the Swedish cookbook history.

SOUPS

~~~

A cauldron over the fire

Soup was for a long time the most common dish in Swedish homes, and the reason was simple: there was usually a cauldron over the fire, and that was where the entire meal was cooked. So most of the food was simply in soup form and included vegetables, root vegetables and meat. The word soup has a Germanic origin and means "pieces of bread dipped in liquid." Soup is related to the Swedish word *supa,* meaning to drink alcohol, as seen in expressions such as "söp soppan" (drank the soup) and "lika goda kålsupare" (equally good cabbage drinkers), which refers to people who eat cabbage soup noisily.

The history behind Sweden's tradition of Thursday pea soup stretches as far back as the Middle Ages. At that time, Sweden was Catholic and the church urged people to fast on Fridays, which meant that they had to avoid meat. Therefore, they made sure to eat their fill the day before with a hefty serving of pea soup with large chunks of pork in it. Peas also belonged to the more luxurious carbohydrates, compared to turnips, while pork was something they ate frequently. Thought that's how the tradition of eating pea soup on Thursdays began, the *punsch* and the pancakes were added later.

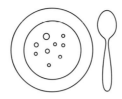

I always serve soup as a starter for lunch at my restaurant. It is the best way to deal with the restaurateur's greatest enemy, the guest's low blood sugar. When a guest arrives at a restaurant, she or he has often fasted a little before. Who wants to go to a restaurant and not be hungry? The problem then is that the guest usually has very little patience. Therefore, serving a soup right away is a great way to satisfy that hunger and get a more satisfied guest who then does not feel that things are slow just because his or her stomach is growling.

Soup is also one of the easiest dishes to cook and is incredibly easy to vary with seasonal foods or with all kinds of scraps from fish and meat. A friend of mine, who is an artist and often uses soups as a motif for his art, feels that soup has a soul, and he is always looking for it wherever he goes. He's absolutely right, for wherever you travel in the world, there is always a variation on a soup: Spanish, Russian and Japanese chefs proudly share their soups. We Swedes should also be proud of our soups and look for our soup souls.

MEAT SOUP

5.5 lbs (2.5 kg) coarsely diced
beef (brisket)
1.7 gallon (6.5 liters) of cold
water
3 carrots
3 leeks
2 onions
2 parsnips
½ celeriac
2 thyme sprigs
1 bay leaf
5 black peppercorns
salt

This recipe is inspired by Modärn kokbok, *which offers poor instructions. I make my soup in a little different way, with fresh thyme and bay leaves instead of dried spices like cloves.*

Bring the beef and water to a boil, skim off any foam carefully.

Peel and cut the vegetables into coarse pieces, tie the thyme and bay leaf together with kitchen twine, put the peppercorns in a tea strainer, and add them when the water has come to a boil.

Reduce temperature and let the soup simmer for 4–5 hours, season the soup with salt, and lift up the tea strainer with the peppercorns and the bundle of herbs.

Serve the soup with dumplings.

POINTED CABBAGE SOUP

Cabbage soup is a dish that many people might think is a little boring, and may be considered a poor man's food. It is inexpensive food but very good! I make mine on pointed cabbage, but regular cabbage works fine. Old recipes for this kind of soup can be found in Modärn kokbok.

Remove the outer leaves, the steam, and the coarsest leaves of the cabbage. Cut it into pieces and cook in a wide saucepan with some butter.

Add the syrup and stir carefully so that the sugar in the syrup won't burn.

Heat the stock and pour over the cabbage. Add the split as pepper-corns and cook until the cabbage is soft.

Season the soup with salt and pepper, and serve with boiled and fried pork cut in slices.

10.5 cups (2.5 liters) stock
1 head of pointed cabbage
2 tablespoons butter
1 tablespoon syrup
a few allspice kernels
salt
white pepper

FISH SOUP WITH TOMATOES FROM VIKEN

8.5 cups (2 liters) water
4.4 lbs (2 kg) white lean fish
1 tablespoon salt
2 carrots
1 parsnip
1 piece of celery root
1 fennel
1 container mixed fresh tomatoes
(Ideally from Viken, Sweden)
1 scant cup (200 ml) tomato
juice
1 small bunch parsley
1 bay leaf
8 white peppercorns
1 tablespoon butter

"Ocean fish provide the best broth, mackerel and fresh herring, the fattiest. The cooked fish can be used for fish soufflé."

*–Husmoderns kokbok
(The Housewife's Cookbook)*

I cook my broth the classic way with the bones in, but I like to have the fish in the soup. Let the fish finish cooking in the clear broth when the soup is almost done.

Clean the fish, rinse it well and cut it in pieces. Tie bay leaves and parsley together with twine. Add fish bones, white pepper and herbs in a saucepan with cold water and salt. Save the fish for later.

Bring everything to a boil and skim off foam after it first comes to a boil. Cook another 15 minutes and strain off the bones.

Peel and cut the root vegetables into rough pieces. Fry them in butter in another saucepan and add the broth. Pour in tomato juice and let the soup cook until the root vegetables become soft.

Add the fish and the tomatoes and cook for the last 5 minutes on very low heat.

OXTAIL SOUP

In many old recipes clear soups are thickened with egg yolk or butter and flour. When I was looking for inspiration for this book and looked at old cookbooks (including Husmoderns kokbok)*, there were several recipes that were called* Afhvredd *(thickened) oxtail soup, but I read it as "Alfred's oxtail soup" ... A little funny, but I choose to make my soup without any thickening. Oxtail makes a particularly good broth and it's a shame to ruin it.*

Wash the oxtail with water and dry it well. (One usually buys chopped oxtail; you can ask your butcher to do it for you.)

Cut the root vegetables and onion into pieces.

Fry the butter in a saucepan and brown the tailpieces. Add the water and cook slowly for 2–3 hours with half of the root vegetables, onion and pepper and parsley, until the meat separates from the bones.

Strain the broth into another pot and pick the meat off the bones while they are still hot, which makes it easier. Let the broth reduce slightly and add the remaining roots and onions, and cook until tender. Add the oxtail meat, and season the soup with sherry, salt, and pepper, and if you like a knob of butter.

10.5 cups (2.5 liters) water
1 oxtail
1 knob of butter
1 small shallot
1 carrot
1 parsnip
8–10 allspice kernels
3 sprigs parsley
salt
white peppercorns
½ cup (100 ml) sherry

CONSOMMÉ

STOCK

3 chicken carcasses
1.1 lb (500 g) veal bones or
oxtail
2 onions
2 carrots
½ celeriac
6 black peppercorns
2 thyme sprigs
1 bay leaf

CONSOMMÉ

salt
pepper
sherry vinegar
any meat saved from the bones

You can make consommé, which is a clear broth that is served very hot, out of all kinds of meat. A common way to clarify broth used to be to whip egg whites in hot broth, which then coagulates and attracts the protein and fat. I do it a little bit differently.

Wash the carcasses thoroughly and remove as much fat and meat scraps you can.

Roast them in the oven at 480°F (250°C) until they are quite browned.

Remove them from the oven and put them in a large pot, fill it with water and let it come to a boil. Skim off the stock carefully, and then lower the temperature.

Peel and cut the vegetables into rough pieces and add them along with the herbs and spices. Let cook for 2–3 hours.

Strain the broth and let it reduce until about ⅔ remains.

Cool the finished broth in a jar or container and place it in the freezer. When you want to make consommé, take it out and thaw it in the refrigerator in a strainer lined with a coffee filter or cheesecloth. The liquid melts first, and the fat and protein stay in the filter.

Heat up the consommé and season with salt, pepper, sherry, and vinegar. If you like, serve with a little meat.

5. *Consommé*

6. Spinach soup

CREAM *For commoners, cream was primarily a commodity that was churned to make butter. Butter was a method of preserving fat from milk during the winter months. In northern Sweden, they poured the milk in a dish and let it sit for three days. The cream settled like a thick film on top of the milk, and it could easily be separated from the milk by holding down the cream with a wooden stick. Since the cream had by then become sour, sour cream is commonly seen in their recipes.*

MILK *Milk was one of the farm's most important products and was only available in summer. Most often people preserved it by churning it into butter or making cheese out of it. Both of these dairy products could be sold on the market to bring in some money to the farm. Older generations considered it a waste to actually drink the sweet milk. Eventually, people learned another way of extending the milk's life, namely by adding a culture—what we today call yogurt and buttermilk. This they could drink without a guilty conscience.*

SPINACH SOUP

Chop the garlic and onion and cook in the oil. Add the broth and cook till reduced to half the amount. Add the cream and cook another 5 minutes.

Just before serving, add the spinach and mix together to a creamy soup. Season to taste with salt and pepper. Serve with creamy eggs (see recipe on page 239).

3.5 oz (100 g) spinach leaves
1 cup (250 ml) cream
1 cup (250 ml) chicken stock
1 onion
1 clove of garlic
oil for cooking
salt and pepper

ASPARAGUS SOUP

14 oz (400 g) asparagus (peels and stems that you have cut off and saved)
1 onion
1 clove garlic
zest of 1 lemon
1 scant cup (200 ml) chicken broth
1 scant cup (200 ml) white wine
1¾ cups (400 ml) cream
a pinch of sugar
a pinch of salt
champagne vinegar
1 knob of butter

This is a perfect soup to make from asparagus peels. If you want to cook this in the winter, you can use frozen green asparagus, but the peel from the white asparagus is the best.

Peel and chop the onion and garlic finely, and fry it in a pan with a little oil. Add the asparagus and lemon zest.

Add the stock and white wine, and water, if needed, so that the asparagus is covered, and cook for about 20 minutes.

Add the cream and cook for another 5 minutes.

Blend the soup thoroughly in a blender or with an immersion blender.

Strain it and season with a little sugar, salt, and a dash of vinegar.

Mix in a dollop of butter with an immersion blender just before serving.

PEA SOUP

Check the peas for debris and let them soak overnight.

Place in a saucepan with 8.5 cups (2 liters) of water.

When it comes to a boil, skim and remove skins that rise to the top. Add the pork and the whole onion. Allow the soup to boil with the lid closed about 3 hours until the peas are completely soft.

Remove the pork and season the soup with salt. Cut the pork into pieces and put it back into the soup. Serve with home-made mustard.

2 cups (500 ml) yellow peas, whole
8.5 cups (2 liters) water
14 oz (400 g) salt-cured, thick-cut bacon
1 yellow onion
salt

PUNSCH comes from the Sanskrit word *pancha,* meaning five. It's thought that the name stems from the fact that you can count the ingredients on one hand: alcohol, water, sugar, lemon juice, and tea. In Swedish home-style cooking, punsch has tradition-ally ended the typical Thursday dinner of pea soup. The meal was made a little more luxurious with hot punsch! Swedish author August Strindberg is believed to have been very fond punsch.

CRAYFISH SOUP

2.2 lbs (1 kg) crayfish
2 carrots
2 onions
1 fennel
1 teaspoon dill seeds
1 teaspoon fennel seeds
¼ cup (50 ml) tomato paste
1¾ cup (400 ml) white wine
2 cups (500 ml) cream
¼ cup (50 ml) cognac
sherry vinegar
salt
pepper

Shell the crayfish and save the flesh. Save the shells from the tails and the backs.

Peel and cut the vegetables into rough chunks.

Lay crayfish shells and vegetables on a baking sheet. Add the tomato paste and mix.

Roast it in the oven at 355°F (180°C) degrees for about 15 minutes.

When the shells are completely dry, put them in a saucepan and add the wine. Cover the shells with water. Add the fennel seeds and dill seeds. Let the stock boil for about 20 minutes and skim off in the meantime. Strain off shells and vegetables, and return the stock to the pan.

Reduce even more for about 20 minutes until two thirds remains.

Add cream and cook for about another 10 minutes.

Season soup with salt, pepper, and cognac, and regulate the acidity with sherry vinegar.

Mix lightly with an immersion blender and serve the soup with the flesh of the crayfish.

9. Crayfish soup

POTATO AND LEEK SOUP

2 leeks
14 oz (400 g) mealy potatoes
2 garlic cloves
1½ cups (300 ml) white wine
1½ cups (300 ml) chicken broth
water
salt and pepper
1 knob of butter
crème fraiche

Rinse leeks thoroughly and cut them into pieces. Do not use too much of the green, but slice the green thinly and place in cold water; use this to top the soup with just before serving. Peel and cut potatoes into rough chunks.

Fry the leeks in a little oil in a saucepan until translucent, then add the potatoes.

Add the broth and wine, and add enough water to cover potatoes.

Add salt, and cook until the potatoes are thoroughly soft.

Blend the soup with an immersion blender and season with salt and pepper, add the butter and mix some more. Add a little water if needed.

Serve the soup with the finely cut green leek and a dollop of crème fraiche.

MUSHROOM SOUP

Mushroom soup is absolutely delicious and can be made with most kinds of mushrooms. Use whatever mushrooms are in season, or use dried mushrooms that you soak in warm water for about 5 minutes and then drain.

Clean the mushrooms, peel and chop the onion and garlic. Cook everything in a little oil in a large saucepan. Add the wine and stock, and cook for about 20 minutes.

Add the cream and cook for another 5 minutes.

Blend the soup thoroughly and season with salt, pepper, sherry, and port.

14 oz (400 g) of mushrooms, any that are in season
2 onions
2 cloves garlic
water
1 scant cup (200 ml) white wine
1 scant cup (200 ml) chicken or light veal stock
1½ cup (300 ml) cream
salt and freshly-ground black pepper
sherry
port wine

13. Mustard

VÄSTERBOTTEN CRISPS

Shred Västerbotten cheese finely and put on a baking sheet lined with parchment paper.

Bake in oven at 350°F (175°C) for 5–10 minutes until cheese is golden brown color.

Remove the baking sheet and let the cheese set.

Break the cheese crisp in to irregular pieces and serve with your favorite soup.

3.5 oz (100 g) Västerbotten cheese

MUSTARD

Pour water into three pans, and bring to a boil in all three.

When they boil, pour the mustard seeds in a strainer and then blanch them in all three pots. Do this by dipping the strainer down quickly in the first pot and then brining it out, and then dip it in the next, take it

up again, and finally dip it into the third pot. This is done to make the flavor milder.

Then place all ingredients in a blender and blend together into a creamy mustard. Season with salt, and, if needed, some more vinegar and honey.

3.5 oz (100 grams) mustard seeds (black and yellow)
3 tablespoons apple cider vinegar
2 tablespoons honey
½ cup (100 ml) oil
3 figs
1 pinch salt
salt

CROUTONS

1 chunk of yesterday's bread
(any bread will do)
3 tablespoons cold-pressed
rapeseed oil or butter
a pinch of salt
freshly ground black pepper

Cut the bread into thin slices or squares. It is easier if the bread has been frozen.

Lay the croutons on a baking sheet and drizzle with oil or dab with butter. Season with salt and pepper.

Roast the croutons in the oven at 350°F (175°C) for 5–10 minutes until they have a golden-brown color. Serve the croutons as a topping for soup or salad.

DUMPLINGS

2 cups (500 ml) flour
1 scant cup (200 ml) milk
1 egg
1 pinch salt

Boil a large pot of salted water.

Mix all ingredients for the dumplings into a smooth batter.

Drop the batter into boiling water using two spoons.

Cook the dumplings until they float to the surface and then lift them out with a slotted spoon and serve with meat soup.

15. Dumplings

FISH

"Herring soup" for breakfast

One evening in 1929, a high society woman named Elvira invited her girlfriends over for dinner. The dinner was a tasty and creamy anchovy dish with potatoes, onions, and cream. But Elvira thought the dish needed to be spruced up with a fun name, and thought of a silent movie that she had seen a year earlier in one of Stockholm's movie theatres. The film was called Jansson's Temptation, which she thought was appropriate for the tasty fish dish, so she gave this name to her anchovies au gratin.

Seafood has historically been an important source of protein, both for those who lived along the coast and for those who lived inland. Most common for most households was the salted herring. In less fortunate homes it would be eaten for breakfast in a "herring soup" or with a piece of bread, and in better-off families and on special occasions it was eaten with different pickles in vinegar. Fancier fish included turbot, salmon, cod, plaice, and flounder; it was considered particularly fancy to eat cod tongues and pike livers.

In the 1800s, people began to open their eyes to crayfish. When Europe's finest restaurants decided that it was a delicacy, the Swedes took full advantage. With lakes full of shellfish, for a few decades Sweden became the world's leading crayfish exporter. But the booming exports came to an abrupt end in 1907, when Finnish-imported crayfish infected the Swedish crayfish with the so-called crayfish plague. After World War II, Swedes, missing their traditional late-summer crayfish, reversed roles and became the biggest importers of crayfish.

How does one determine if the fish is good? There is a simple rule to stick to and that is to rely on your sense of smell—if the fish smells good, it is good, and if it has a questionable or even bad smell, then it should probably be thrown out. When checking the freshness of a fish, look at three things: eyes, gills, and skin mucus. To increase durability, a fish should be cleaned instantly after being caught, and it should be kept well chilled. Most fish should be consumed fresh, but some, like plaice halibut, and sole, are similar to meat and get even better if they are allowed to rest for some weeks.

Fish is a sore subject today. Oceans are being overfished and many fish risk total extinction. However, fish remains an incredibly important part of our culinary tradition. Many of Sweden's major holidays are based on different types of pickled fish. I myself think that fish is really good!

If you want to make sure that you eat the right kind of fish, you can check the World Wildlife Fund (WWF) website, which has a guide for which fish are sustainable and what seafood should be avoided.

Eating fish in-season is also important. Many Swedes have succeeded well in mostly eating our beloved seafood in the right season, and thus we have kept the stock stable and vibrant, but it would be wonderful if we could see more of this kind of thinking about all kinds of fish. It is also sometimes niceto have something to look forward to! The long wait for Easter herring, August crayfish, and Christmas lutefish can be just lovely!

The fish recipes in this book are recipes that my chefs and I have tested out at my restaurant, Restaurang 1900, as well as recipes that I've often cooked at home for various Swedish holidays, or for everyday use.

17. Classic pickled herring   *24. Juniper berry herring*   *18. Fennel herring*

20. Shallot herring   *27. Sea buckthorn herring*   *19. Pink pepper and lemon herring*

BASIC PICKLING BRINE FOR HERRING

Cook all ingredients except the herring in a saucepan on the stove.

Pour it into another container and let it cool down and keep the brine in the refrigerator.

Rinse salted herring fillets under cold running water for about 20 minutes.

Place them in a clean container and add cold brine over the herring to cover it. Save the rest of the brine.

Put something on it to press it down, for example a lid from a small jar. Let sit for one day in the refrigerator.

Lift up the herring fillets and cut them into pieces. Be sure to have clean hands or gloves to increase durability.

Add herring pieces in a new, clean container and add a new brine to cover the herring. Let sit for another day.

After 24 hours, you have a pickled herring, which can be flavored in many ways. It will keep for about a month in the refrigerator.

3 cups (700 ml) water
1.1 lb (500 g) sugar
1 scant cup (200 ml) vinegar
5 allspice kernels
2 bay leaves
10 salted herring fillets

CLASSIC PICKLED HERRING

14 oz (400 g) basic pickled
herring

BRINE
½ leeks
3 carrots
1 onion
2 cups (500 ml) of strained
herring brine

Place the herring in a jar.

Wash the leek and slice it. Peel the carrots and onions. Cut the carrot in coins and the onion into rough pieces. Add both to the herring.

Pour the brine on top and let it sit for at least 6 hours in the refrigerator.

FENNEL HERRING

14 oz (400 g) basic pickled
herring

BRINE
2 fennel bulbs
1 tablespoon fennel seeds
2 cups (500 ml) of strained
herring brine

Slice the fennel thinly and place it along with the herring in a jar.

Toast the fennel seeds in a dry skillet until they snap, but before they brown.

Add the toasted fennel seeds and pour the cold herring brine on top.

Refrigerate at least 6 hours.

PINK PEPPER AND LEMON HERRING

Wash the lemons and peel away the outer zest without any pith.

Cut the flesh without hitting any white membranes.

Squeeze the remaining juice from the lemon. Crush the pink peppercorns.

Boil the lemon zest and pink peppercorns with the herring brine. Add the flesh from the lemon as well as the lemon juice. Let the brine cool down.

Place the herring in a jar and add the cold brine.

Let it sit for about 6 hours in the refrigerator and it will be ready to serve.

14 oz (400 g) basic pickled herring

BRINE
5 lemons
¼ cup (50 ml) pink peppercorns
2 cups (500 ml) strained herring brine

SHALLOT HERRING

Place the herring in a jar.

Peel and slice the shallots, add to the jar.

Add cold herring brine and let sit for about 6 hours in the refrigerator before serving.

14 oz (400 g) basic pickled herring

BRINE
4 shallots
2 cups (500 ml) of strained herring brine

RAMPS AND APPLE HERRING

14 oz (400 g) basic pickled
herring

SAUCE
1 scant cup (200 ml) mayonnaise
1 scant cup (200 ml) sour cream
2 tart green apples
1 bunch ramps
1 pinch of salt
freshly ground white pepper

Grate the apple coarsely and chop the ramps finely.

Mix with mayonnaise and sour cream, and season with salt and pepper.

Mix the sauce with the herring and place in a jar, at least 6 hours before serving.

HERRING WITH HERBS

14 oz (400 g) basic pickled
herring

SAUCE
1 scant cup (200 ml) crème
fraiche
1 scant cup (200 ml) mayonnaise
1 bunch dill
1 bunch parsley
1 lemon
a pinch of salt
freshly ground white pepper

Chop the herbs coarsely, grate the zest of the lemon and squeeze out the juice.

Mix herbs, lemon juice, and zest with crème fraiche in a food processor, to a light green color.

Mix the sauce with the mayonnaise and season with salt and white pepper.

Mix the sauce with the herring and place in a jar for at least 6 hours before serving.

26. Herring from Ingarö

21. Ramps and apple herring

23. Tomato and sherry herring

22 Herring with herbs

25. Grandfather's herring

28. Mustard herring

TOMATO AND SHERRY HERRING

14 oz (400 g) basic pickled herring

SAUCE
1 can of whole blanched tomatoes about 15 oz (200g)
1 onion
1 clove garlic
3 tablespoons sherry vinegar
2 tablespoons brown sugar
4 tablespoons dry sherry
¼ cup (50 ml) olive oil
a pinch of salt
freshly ground black pepper

Chop the onion and garlic finely, and fry them till translucent in a pan with a little oil.

Add the tomatoes, and cook everything for about 15 minutes.

Add some water if needed and season the sauce with vinegar, sherry, sugar, salt, pepper, and olive oil.

Chill the sauce, and then mix in the herring.

Keep in a jar for at least 6 hours before serving.

JUNIPER BERRY HERRING

400 basic pickled herring

BRINE
¼ cup (50 ml) dried juniper berries
2 cups (500 ml) strained herring brine

Place herring and juniper in a jar. Add herring brine and refrigerate for at least 6 hours before the herring is served.

GRANDFATHER'S HERRING

The real name of this herring is Dad's herring, but we renamed it after our former head chef at Restaurang 1900, whom we called Grandpa because he was the oldest one there. More specifically, two years older than me . . .

Rinse the matjes fillets in cold water to remove some of the salt and the red color.

Allow them to dry in a strainer or on a paper towel. Cut them into ¾ inch (2 cm) pieces.

Chop the dill and chives finely. Mix all ingredients for the sauce and season.

Mix with the herring and place in a jar for at least 6 hours before serving.

10 matjes herring fillets

SAUCE
7 fl oz (200 g) mayonnaise
1 scant cup (200 ml) sour cream
2 tablespoons sugar
1 bunch dill
1 bunch chives
freshly ground white pepper

HERRING FROM INGARÖ

Mix all ingredients for the sauce and season with salt and pepper.

Mix the sauce with the herring, and store in a jar for at least 6 hours before serving.

14 oz (400 g) basic pickled herring

SAUCE
1½ cup (300 ml) mayonnaise
1½ cup (300 ml) sour cream
3.5 oz (100 grams) any kind of roe, such as bleak roe
1 pinch salt
freshly ground white pepper

SEA BUCKTHORN HERRING

14 oz (400 g) basic pickled
herring

BRINE
1 scant cup (200 ml) frozen sea
buckthorn berries (or fresh if
you can get it)
2 cups (500 ml) of strained
herring brine

Place herring and sea buckthorn in a jar.

Add herring brine and refrigerate for 6 hours or so, and
the herring will be ready to be
served.

For additional flavor, add
spruce tips. In late summer you
can pick them and flavor the
herring with them—the flavor
marries perfectly with the sea
buckthorn and contributes to a
nice green color.

MUSTARD HERRING

14 oz (400 g) basic pickled
herring

SAUCE
1 yellow onion
½ cup (100 ml) white wine
vinegar
½ cup (100 ml) Skåne mustard*
¼ cup (50 ml) Dijon mustard
1 scant cup (200 ml) sugar
1 scant cup (200 ml) cooking oil
about ½ cup (100 ml) crème
fraiche
a pinch of salt
freshly ground white pepper

Chop the onion finely and mix
it with vinegar, mustard, and
sugar.

Pour the oil in very slowly
while whisking.

Mix in crème fraiche, and season with salt and white pepper.

Mix the sauce with the herring,
and store in a jar for at least
6 hours before serving.

*note: Skåne mustard is a typical
Swedish condiment that can
be purchased at specialty food
stores, IKEA, and online.

MAYONNAISE

Most creamy herrings and sauces are based on mayonnaise. It will taste best if you make it yourself.

Place egg yolks, salt, vinegar, and mustard in a food processor. Mix together.

Pour the oil in very slowly until the mayonnaise is very thick; you may not need all the oil, or you may need a little more. (With more acidity and salt, you will need more oil and thus get a thicker mayonnaise.)

Season with salt. Store in a clean container in the refrigerator. Mayonnaise will keep up to 3 weeks.

3 egg yolks
2 tablespoons white wine vinegar
2 tablespoons Dijon mustard
a pinch of salt
about 5 cups (1200 ml) oil

30. Aged matjes herring with browned butter and potatoes

AGED MATJES HERRING WITH BROWNED BUTTER AND POTATOES

Extra aged matjes herring, which is available from your fishmonger, has been aged for a year and has a stronger flavor than regular pickled herring.

Cut the herring into small pieces and leave them out to reach room temperature.

Wash the potatoes and boil them in salted water.

Chop the onions finely and cut the chives into thin rings.

Melt the butter in a saucepan and let it brown until you smell a sweet and nutty aroma, and the proteins in the butter have a golden-brown color.

Arrange the herrings on a plate with potatoes, red onions, and chives, and add warm melted butter over the fish just before serving.

4 extra aged Matjes herring fillets
8 potatoes of a waxy kind
2 red onions
1 bunch of chives
7 oz (200 g) butter

FRIED BALTIC HERRING

24 Baltic herring fillets
coarse rye flour
salt and white pepper
butter and oil to fry in

Cut away the dorsal fin from the herrings. Arrange all the fillets with the flesh side up.

Add salt and pepper, and assemble them in pairs with flesh sides together.

Dredge them in coarse rye flour.

Fry herrings in oil in a hot pan, about 2 minutes on each side. Dab with plenty of butter towards the end, and baste them with the liquids for a delicious browned butter flavor and a crispy surface.

FRIED PICKLED HERRING

12 servings fried herring

BRINE
¼ cup (50 ml) vinegar
½ cup (100 ml) sugar
¾ cup (150 ml) water
1 carrot
1 onion
3 bay leaves

Place the fried herrings in a baking dish or a plastic container.

Boil the water and add the vinegar and sugar. Whisk until the sugar dissolves.

Peel and cut the carrot and onion into rough pieces and add them along with the bay leaves to the brine.

Chill the brine, and then pour it over the herring. Store in the refrigerator and let sit at least 6 hours before serving. Serve the herring for a herring smorgasbord, or with boiled potatoes and sour cream.

33. Baltic herring casserole with sandwich caviar
34. Baltic herring à la crayfish

BALTIC HERRING CASSEROLE WITH SANDWICH CAVIAR

Grease an ovenproof dish and cut off the dorsal fin from herring fillets. Roll them with the flesh side inwards and place them tightly against each other in the dish. Add salt and pepper.

Chop the onion finely and cook it with cream. Season with the sandwich caviar, salt, and white pepper.

Pour the sauce over the herring and bake in the oven at 400°F (200°C) for about 15 minutes.

Serve the herring casserole cold for a buffet or as a separate dish along with boiled potatoes and lemon.

1.1 lb (500 g) herring fillets

SAUCE
¼ cup (50 ml) sandwich caviar (creamed smoked cod roe spread)
1¼ cup (250 ml) cream
1 small onion
salt and freshly ground white pepper

BALTIC HERRING À LA CRAYFISH

1.1 lb (500 g) herring fillets

SAUCE
1¼ cup (250 ml) tomato juice
8 oz (230 g) tomato paste
1 scant cup (200 ml) water
1 teaspoon dill seeds
1⅛ cup (130 ml) sugar
⅜ cup (75 ml) vinegar
1 bunch dill
salt and freshly ground white pepper

This herring casserole really has nothing to do with crayfish, except that it is flavored with dill seeds and dill just like you would flavor freshwater crayfish. Along with the sweetness of the tomato, the lightly salted herring is a wonderful dish that will remind you of a crayfish party in August.

Chop the dill finely and save stems.

Cut away the dorsal fins from the herring fillets, roll them with the flesh side inwards and place the rolls in a greased ovenproof dish, season with salt and pepper.

Cook all ingredients for the sauce except the chopped dill; the dill stems should cook with everything else, bound together with cooking twine.

Let the sauce reduce until about ⅔ remains. Lift up the dill stalks and season with salt and white pepper.

Pour the sauce over the herring and bake the casserole in the oven at 400°F (200°C) for about 15 minutes.

Serve crayfish herring as a buffet dish or with boiled potatoes for a delicious lunch dish.

JANSSON'S TEMPTATION

Wash and cut potatoes into juliennes, and peel and cut the onion into rings.

Grease an ovenproof dish and alternate potatoes, onions and anchovies. Season with salt and white pepper, but be careful with the salt because the fish is already quite salty.

Pour a little of the brine from the anchovies, as well as the cream and the milk.

Sprinkle a thin layer of breadcrumbs on top and bake the casserole in the oven at 350°F (175°C) for about 30 minutes until the potatoes are thoroughly soft and the casserole has got a nice golden-brown color. If it is brown but the potato feels hard, cover the pan with foil to prevent it from burning.

2.2 lbs (1 kg) potatoes
3 onions
1 can of anchovies
1¾ cup (400 ml) cream
1 scant cup (200 ml) milk
salt and freshly ground white
* pepper*
½ cup (100 ml) bread crumbs

POACHED SALMON WITH GINGER

1.3 lbs (600 g) salmon

1 scant cup (200 ml) water
½ cup (100 ml) sugar
⅜ cup (75 ml) vinegar
1 tablespoon + 2 teaspoons lemon juice
1 onion
1 carrot
3 pieces of dried ginger

Cut the salmon into serving sizes, and place the pieces in an ovenproof form. Place a thermometer into one of the salmon fillets. Boil water, sugar, and vinegar into a brine.

Peel and cut the onion and carrot into rough pieces and put them in the brine together with the ginger. Add the lemon juice.

Pour the warm brine over the salmon, and cover the form with plastic or foil. Leave the form out in a warm place in the kitchen until the salmon has an internal temperature of 107°F (42°C). Take the salmon out of the brine and serve immediately, or let cool and serve as a dish for a buffet. The salmon can be kept warm for a while in the oven at 122°F (50°C), if you want to serve it warm.

SEARED SALMON

1.3 lbs (600 g) salted salmon
oil for cooking

Cut the salmon into portion sizes, about 5 oz (150 g) per person.

Heat a cast iron pan on the stove, making sure it is really hot.

Pour in a little oil and put the salmon in with the flesh side down. Sear for about 4 minutes, then place the salmon on a baking sheet. Serve the salmon as is, salted and seared, or cook through in the oven at 212°F (100°C) to a 107°F (42°C) internal temperature.

OVEN-BAKED SALMON WITH PARSLEY ROOT

Preheat oven to 400°F (200°C) degrees. Scrub and halve parsley roots lengthwise.

Cut the salmon into individual servings, about 5 oz (150 g) per person. Sprinkle lightly with salt and pepper, and leave them out on the cutting board while the parsley roots are roasting.

Place the parsley roots on a baking sheet and roast them for about 5 minutes, with a little oil and salt.

Lower the temperature to 212°F (100°C) and put the salmon next to the parsley roots. Finish baking the salmon in the oven till it reaches an internal temperature of 107°F (42°C).

1.3 lbs (600 g) salmon
8 parsley roots
oil
salt and white pepper

SALT-CURED SALMON

Whisk the salt in the water so that it dissolves properly, add the white pepper corns, grate and add the lemon peel. Press the juice from the lemon and add as well.

Remove any bones from salmon and cut off unnecessary fat and skin.

Place salmon skin side down in a deep baking tray and pour over the salt brine. Cure the salmon in a refrigerator for 10 hours.

Remove the salmon from the brine, and dry it thoroughly. Cut into thin slices and serve with creamed dill potatoes.

1 whole side of salmon
½ cup (100 ml) salt
4 cups (1000 ml) water
20 white peppercorns
1 lemon

GRAVLAX WITH RED BEETS

1 whole side of salmon
2.2 lbs (1 kg) red beets
¼ cup (1¾ ounce) (50 g) sugar
3 tablespoons (1¾ ounce)
(50 g) salt
zest of 1 lemon
3 sprigs thyme

Remove any bones from the salmon side and place it on a baking sheet. Wash beets and grate them coarsely.

Mix salt and sugar and sprinkle a thin layer evenly over the salmon. You may need all of it, depending on the size of the fish, but it can be saved more or less indefinitely. (As long as you don't put dirty fingers in it.)

Spread the grated beetroot, thyme sprigs, and finely grated lemon peel over the salmon and rub thoroughly.

Let the salmon sit at room temperature until sugar and salt has melted and starts to form a liquid on the plate. Add the salmon with the flesh side down and leave in the refrigerator for at least 12 hours.

Lift the salmon and scrape off the beetroot, lemon zest, and thyme. Rinse the salmon quickly under cold water, and place it on a clean tray or plate.

40. Gravlax with red beets

41. Trout in foil packet

TROUT IN FOIL PACKET

Place each trout on a large piece of aluminum foil. Add salt and pepper all over.

Cut vegetables and lemon in slices and put them on top of and all around the fish. Crush the fennel seeds lightly and sprinkle on top. Add a knob of butter to each packet.

Bake in the oven at 400°F (200°C) or grill with the lid on for about 15 minutes.

Eat straight from the packet with some boiled potatoes, or just as is.

2 trout, cleaned and gutted
1 fennel bulb
20 fennel seeds
1 yellow onion
2 lemons
salt and white pepper
3.5 oz (100g) butter

CHAR TERRINE

4.4 lbs (2 kg) char fillet, with-
out skins and bones
¼ cup (1¾ ounce) (50 g) sugar
3 tablespoons (1¾ ounce)
(50 g) salt
freshly ground white pepper
zest of 1 lemon
2 cups (500 ml) white wine
2½ cups (600 ml) water
1 onion
6 dill seeds
12 leaves of gelatin

Mix salt and sugar with white pepper and sprinkle it evenly over trout fillets that have been placed on a baking sheet.

Let the fish cure at room temperature for about 30 minutes.

Boil the water and wine in a saucepan, and let the gelatin leaves soak in cold water.

Peel and cut the onion into rough pieces and add them along with the dill to the pan.

Boil for about 10 minutes, and strain to remove onion and dill.

Add the gelatin to the wine and water mixture and let cool slightly.

Brush a loaf pan with oil, and line the inside with plastic wrap.

Dry the liquid, formed by the salt curing, off the trout fillets, and dip them one by one in the mixture, then put them in the loaf pan. Repeat with all fillets. The wine and gelatin mixture that is left over cannot be saved.

Place plastic wrap over the pan and put another one on top. Put something heavy on top to press down and set the whole thing in the freezer.

Before serving, remove the terrine and allow to thaw slightly for about 30 minutes, and cut into slices or cubes while it is half frozen. Then, let thaw on a platter or plate.

The terrine can be served at a buffet or as an appetizer. The recipe is quite large, but freezes well and will keep up to two months if it is properly sealed in plastic.

Char

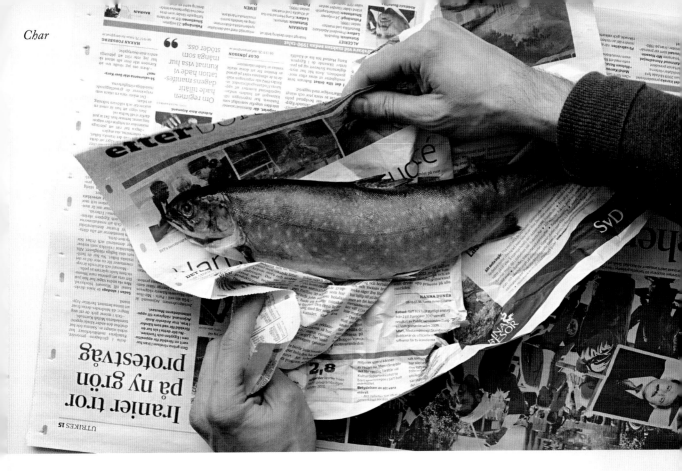

Zander

Greater Weever

European perch

Mackerel

Pike

COD WITH BROWNED BUTTER, SHRIMP, AND HORSERADISH

61.3 lbs (600 g) codfish
salt and freshly ground white
pepper
10.5 oz (300 g) butter
14 oz (400 g) cooked shrimp
1 piece of horseradish

Cut the cod into 5 oz (150 g) portions. Place the pieces flesh side down on a baking sheet, sprinkle with salt and pepper and add a knob of butter on each piece of fish.

Bake in the oven at 300°F (150°C) to an internal temperature of 118°F (48°C).

Put the butter in a saucepan and heat up. Let the butter melt, until it has a sweet nutty smell and you see that the milk protein is starting to get a golden-brown color. Take the pan off the burner, but keep warm until serving.

Peel the shrimp and heat them up in the browned butter without cooking them.

Peel and grate the horse-radish and serve everything with boiled potatoes.

SALT-CURED COD

Mix sugar, salt, and spices thoroughly.

Place the cod on a baking sheet with skin side down.

Sprinkle the sugar and salt mixture over the fish and rub it thoroughly.

Let the fish sit at room temperature until sugar and salt have melted. Turn the cod flesh side down and let it sit in the refrigerator for two days.

Remove the cod from the baking sheet and rinse it quickly in cold water to stop the curing process, then wipe it with a towel.

Serve the cod thinly sliced on a buffet, or as part of an appetizer. Preferably lightly seared.

1.3 lbs (600 g) cod
¼ cup (1¾ ounce) (50 g) sugar
3 tablespoons (1¾ ounce or 50 g) salt
7 dill seeds
8 crushed white peppercorns

FISH BALLS

2.2 lbs (1 kg) of codfish (whole)
4 tablespoons butter
2 eggs
1 scant cup (200 ml) cream
1 tablespoon flour
1 tablespoon salt
freshly ground white pepper
1 tsp sugar
nutmeg

FOR COOKING
fish stock

There are many different kinds of fish balls in older cookbooks, and this one is inspired by a recipe from *Husmoderns Kokbok* (*The Housewife's Cookbook*). The great thing about this particular recipe is that you make the stock and then use it to cook the fish balls in.

Cook stock off the fish bones (in the same way as fish soup with tomatoes, page 18), which the fish balls later will be cooked in.

Mix the fish flesh with butter in a food processor.

Mix flour, cream, spices, and eggs thoroughly, then mix together with ground fish.

Shape the fish balls using two spoons, and cook them in the fish stock.

STEAMED COD

Cut the fish into 5 oz (150 g) portions and remove the skin, season with salt.

Boil water and salt in a large pot with an insert (for example, a pasta pot, or better yet a steam juicer).

Place the cod in the insert and lower it into the saucepan. The water should not reach the fish, it should be steamed till done. Pour out a little water if necessary.

Put on the lid and let steam over low heat on the stove for about 10 minutes.

1.3 lbs (600 g) codfish
2 cups (500 ml) water
salt

47. Cod with egg and anchovy salad

COD WITH EGG AND ANCHOVY SALAD

Melt the butter in a saucepan, then take off the burner and let the white protein sink to the bottom. Carefully pour the clarified butter into another container. Keep warm for serving.

Chop the onion and cook it slowly in the butter until soft, then let it cool. Boil the eggs for 6 minutes and cool them quickly. Chop them into the same size as the onions and do the same with the anchovies.

Mix all ingredients together and season with pepper.

Salt the cod on all sides. Fry it quickly on the skin side in a hot skillet with some oil in. Bake it till done in the oven at 212°F (100°C) to an internal temperature of 107°F (42°C).

Serve the cod with the egg and anchovy salad and melted butter. Good sides dishes would be boiled potatoes and chopped herbs.

COD
4 serving size pieces of cod
salt
oil to fry in

EGG AND ANCHOVY
SALAD
5 anchovy fillets
2 yellow onions
5 boiled eggs
3.5 oz (100g) butter
freshly ground black pepper

CLARIFIED BUTTER
7 oz (200g) unsalted butter

MUSTARD AND DILL SAUCE

¼ cup (50 ml) Skåne-style
mustard
1 egg yolk
1 tablespoon sugar
1 pinch salt
freshly ground white pepper
2 teaspoons white wine vinegar
1 scant cup (200 ml) cooking oil
1 bunch of chopped dill

Mix the mustard, egg yolk,
spices, and vinegar.

Add the oil in a thin stream
whilst vigorously whisking by
hand.

Add the chopped dill just
before serving.

CHIVE SAUCE

½ cup (100 ml) sour cream
½ cup (100 ml) mayonnaise
1 bunch chopped chives
1 pinch salt
1 pinch sugar
freshly ground white pepper

Mix all ingredients, and add
the chives just before serving.

48. Mustard and dill sauce

49. Chive sauce

50. Cold sauce with roe

51. Parsley and garlic sauce

COLD SAUCE WITH ROE

½ cup (100 ml) crème fraiche
½ cup (100 ml) mayonnaise
2 tablespoons roe, preferably
bleak roe from Kalix
1 pinch salt
1 pinch sugar
freshly ground white pepper

Mix all ingredients in a bowl
and serve.

PARSLEY AND GARLIC SAUCE

1 bunch parsley
1 small clove garlic
1 scant cup (200 ml) smetana
or crème fraiche
½ lemon, juiced
salt and freshly ground white
pepper

Wash and chop the parsley
finely, crush the garlic and mix
with the smetana. Add lemon
juice, salt, and pepper.

REMOULADE

Peel and chop the onion finely. Mix pickles and capers coarsely in food processor by pulsing them. Allow them to drain in a fine sieve to remove excess fluid.

Fry the curry and onions in a little oil in a frying pan and let cool. Mix all ingredients and season with white pepper and maybe some salt, keeping in mind that the capers and pickles are already very salty.

3.5 oz (100 grams) pickles
1 oz (30 g) capers
1 chopped onion
1 teaspoon curry powder
1 scant cup (200 ml) mayonnaise
salt, if needed
freshly ground white pepper
oil for cooking

COLD DILL SAUCE

Chop the dill finely and mix with mayonnaise and smetana.

Season the sauce with salt, sugar, and white pepper.

½ cup (100 ml) mayonnaise
½ cup (100 ml) smetana
a pinch of salt
a pinch of sugar
freshly ground white pepper
1 bunch dill

52. *Remoulade*

53. *Cold dill sauce*

54. *Emulsion sauce with browned butter*

55. *Sauce with Kalle's caviar*

EMULSION SAUCE WITH BROWNED BUTTER

Boil the eggs for 2 minutes, and cool them somewhat in cold water.

Melt butter in a saucepan on the stove and let it brown until it has a sweet and nutty aroma and until the protein has a golden-brown color.

Remove the pan from the stove and let the butter cool to room temperature.

Break the 2-minute eggs in a measuring cup, scrape them out with a teaspoon, and add salt and lemon juice.

Mix in the butter in a thin stream with an immersion blender to make a thick sauce, and dilute it with some milk. This sauce is an emulsion sauce, like hollandaise and béarnaise, but should be slightly thinner.

2 eggs
2 tbsp lemon juice
10.5 oz (300 g) butter
a pinch of salt
a dash of milk

KALLE'S CAVIAR SAUCE

Mix all ingredients and season with pepper, sugar, and salt, but be careful with the salt as the caviar is very salty in itself.

½ cup (100 ml) mayonnaise
½ cup (100 ml) crème fraiche
2 tablespoons Kalle's caviar
freshly ground white pepper
a pinch of salt
a pinch of sugar

HOLLANDAISE SAUCE

2 egg yolks
juice of one lemon
10.5 oz (300 g) clarified butter
a pinch of salt

Beat the egg yolks and lemon juice in a saucepan until the mixture thickens.

Remove the pan from the heat and add melted butter while whisking.

Season with salt and perhaps some more lemon.

Cover the saucepan and let the sauce sit by the stove to keep it warm till serving.

56. Hollandaise sauce

POACHED LING

1.3 lbs (600 g) back of the ling, skinned

BRINE
1 scant cup (200 ml) water
½ cup (100 ml) sugar
⅜ cup (75 ml) vinegar
1 onion
1 carrot
2 bay leaves (preferably fresh)
4 allspice kernels
⅛ cup (25 ml) lemon juice

Cut the fish into individual portions and place them on a baking sheet with high edges or an ovenproof form.

Peel and cut the onion and carrot into rough chunks and cook all the ingredients for the brine except the lemon juice.

Add the lemon juice and pour the warm brine over the ling.

Insert a thermometer in one of the fish pieces and wrap the baking sheet carefully with plastic. Allow to stand in a warm place in the kitchen till the fish reaches an internal temperature of 118°F (48°C).

Lift the fish out of the brine and serve the poached ling hot or cold, at a buffet or as a main dish with boiled potatoes, brown butter, and lemon.

OVEN-BAKED PIKEPERCH WITH CREAMED LEEKS

Grease an ovenproof dish and place the filets in it. Sprinkle them with salt and pepper.

Rinse the leeks thoroughly and cut into fine shreds.

Heat milk and cream in a saucepan, melt the butter in another. When the butter is melted, whisk in the flour. Pour in the milk and cream mixture in batches and let it cook, whisking constantly for at least 15 minutes. Season the sauce with freshly ground white pepper, salt, and grated nutmeg.

Place the leeks on the fish and pour the sauce over on top.

Bake in the oven at 350°F (175°C) for about 30 minutes. The fish should have an internal temperature of 118°F (48°C).

1.3 lbs (600 g) of pike-perch, fileted and skinned

CREAMED LEEKS
2 leeks
1 cup (250 ml) milk
1 cup (250 ml) cream
1 tablespoon butter
2 tablespoons flour
1 pinch of salt
freshly ground white pepper
nutmeg

59. Fried European perch

FRIED EUROPEAN PERCH

Clean the fish, rinse them thoroughly, and slit them on both sides with a sharp knife.

Put salt and pepper both on the outside and inside of the fish.

Peel and slice onions, heat a skillet on the stove. Add the oil and fry the fish for four minutes, then fry for another four minutes on the other side. Take the skillet off the stove and add butter, and baste the fish with it.

Take the perch out of the pan and place on a baking sheet or a plate right next to the stove so that it stays warm, or in the oven at 212°F (100°C).

Strain the butter that you cooked in and serve the perch with butter, a wedge of lemon, boiled potatoes, and fresh herbs.

4 medium-sized European perch
1 yellow onion
fresh herbs such as thyme and rosemary
salt and freshly ground white pepper
butter and oil for cooking

QUENELLES OF PIKE

2.2 lbs (1 kg) pike filet
2 eggs
3½ cups (900 ml) heavy cream
2 teaspoons salt
grated nutmeg
freshly ground white pepper
about 1 scant cup (200 ml)
lightly salted water
oil to grease the pan

Cut the pike into small pieces and leave them in a cold place.

Measure the cream and put in a bowl, crack the eggs and put in a separate bowl and set the bowls in a cold place as well.

Take the food processor bowl and set in the freezer for a short time.

Then take everything out and combine the fish and the salt in the food processor. Mix till you have ground fish and add the cream in a thin stream. Beat the eggs and add them. Try to mix as little as possible after this, season the ground fish and form it into eggshapes using two spoons that you dip in water in between.

Place the quenelles on a lightly greased baking sheet and pour a little salt water on the baking sheet.

Bake the quenelles in the oven at 400°F (200°C) for 10 minutes.

WHITING FILLETS WITH TOMATO SAUCE

This recipe was very common a long time ago, and is found in many older cookbooks, including Husmoderns kokbok (The Housewife's Cookbook). *Here's my slightly more modern version.*

Chop the dill and parsley finely, set aside and save the stems.

Marinate the fish with vinegar, salt, lemon juice, white pepper, and stems from the herbs for about 30 minutes.

Meanwhile, cook the sauce. Chop the onion and garlic finely and fry until translucent in a saucepan with olive oil. Add tomatoes, wine, and water so that everything is covered. Let the sauce simmer for about 20 minutes and mix it lightly with an immersion blender.

Season the sauce with salt and freshly ground black pepper.

Lift the fish from the marinade and wipe it lightly. Dredge it in flour and fry in a warm pan with oil for about 3 minutes. Then turn and cook on the other side for another 3 minutes. Remove the pan from the stove and add the butter, and baste the fish with the melted butter for 1 more minute.

Lift out the fish and dry it with a paper towel.

Serve the fried whiting with tomato sauce, chopped herbs, and boiled potatoes.

1.3 lbs (600 g) whiting fillets
1 scant cup (200 ml) flour
butter and oil

MARINADE
1 bunch dill
1 bunch parsley
1 tablespoon vinegar
½ tsp salt
juice of 2 lemons
¼ teaspoon white pepper

TOMATO SAUCE
2 onions
1 clove garlic
½ cup (100 ml) olive oil
2 cans 15 oz (400 ml) whole peeled tomatoes
1 scant cup (200 ml) red wine
water
salt and freshly ground black pepper

STEWED PIKE WITH CRAYFISH TAILS

1 pike
1 onion
3.5 oz (100g) butter
¼ cup (50 ml) flour
2 cups (500 ml) milk
salt
1 bunch dill
1 container crayfish tails

Clean the pike.

Cut the fish straight across the back into steak-like pieces.

Place the steaks in a low sauteuse pan (pan with edges) along with sliced onion and cover with water.

Cook the pike for about 15 minutes until the flesh releases from the bones. Lift it out of the cooking water while you prepare the sauce.

Melt the butter in a saucepan and whisk in the flour. Pour in the milk little by little and cook while whisking briskly. Cook for at least 10 minutes so that the flour taste goes away and so that the sauce will be quite thick. Dilute it if needed with stock from the fish. Season with salt. Chop the dill and stir into the flour mixture.

Heat up the pike in the sauce just before serving, add the crawfish tails to the sauce and serve.

CRAYFISH In the 1800s, people began to open their eyes to crayfish, and, when the best restaurants in Europe named it a delicacy, Swedish farmers took full advantage. With lakes filled with crayfish, for a few decades Sweden became the world's leading exporter of crayfish. But this prosperity came to an abrupt end when the crayfish plague arrived. After World War II, the Swedish reclaimed the tradition of eating crayfish, though now as the country with the biggest crayfish imports.

62. *Stewed pike with crayfish tails*

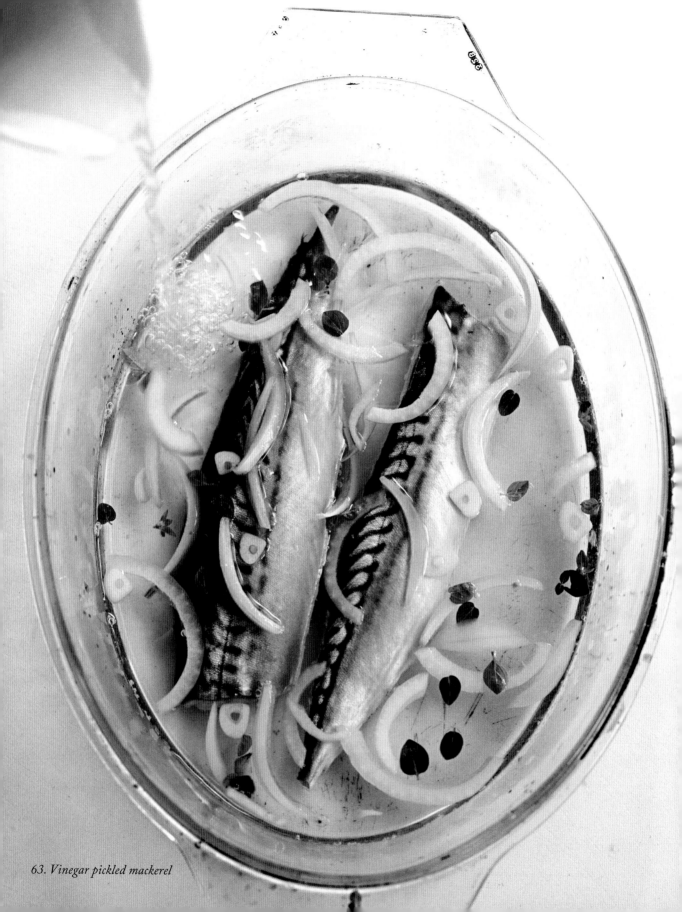

63. Vinegar pickled mackerel

VINEGAR PICKLED MACKEREL

Peel and slice the onion and garlic.

Measure all ingredients for the brine in a saucepan and boil thoroughly.

Cut the mackerel into chunks and place in plastic container that can withstand heat.

Let the brine cool off to 160°F (70°C). Pour it over the mackerel and put a lid on or wrap tightly with plastic wrap.

Let cool to room temperature and put it in the fridge.

Serve the mackerel as a side dish on a buffet or as an appetizer.

8 mackerel fillets
½ cup (100 ml) white wine vinegar
½ cup (100 ml) lemon juice
¾ cup (150 ml) sugar
1½ cup (300 ml) water
1 yellow onion
2 garlic cloves
fresh or dried herbs (use what you have; dill seeds, fennel, thyme, or fresh oregano work well)

BROILED OYSTERS

1 oyster per person
Hollandaise sauce
(See recipe on page 78)

Open the oysters and cut them off from the muscle. Pour off any excess liquid from the shells. Put them in an oven-proof pan or dish.

Add a small dab of hollandaise sauce on each oyster and broil them in the oven at 400°F (200°C), for about 3 minutes.

Serve as an appetizer or on a buffet with an oyster fork.

64. Broiled oysters

65. Cockles with tomato

COCKLES WITH TOMATO

Rinse the mussels in cold water to remove any grit.

Chop tomato, onion, carrot, and fennel.

Cook the vegetables in olive oil until the onion has become translucent.

Add the clams and cover with white wine and put a lid on top.

Let it cook until the mussels open. Discard the mussels that have not opened.

Strain the liquid into another saucepan and reduce until ⅔ remains.

Season with salt and freshly ground black pepper.

Return the mussels to the pan to heat them up. Serve in a bowl with tomato wedges and freshly picked herbs. If you like, drizzle with a good olive oil.

1 bag of cockles
1 tomato
1 onion
1 carrot
½ fennel
olive oil
white wine
salt
freshly ground black pepper

FISH PUDDING

14 oz (400 g) of cured fish (for example cod or salt-cured salmon)
2.2 lbs (1 kg) potatoes
3 onions
4 cups (1000 ml) cream
1½ cups (300 ml) milk
salt
freshly ground white pepper
1 bunch dill

Slice the fish thinly and chop the dill.

Peel and cut potatoes into thin slices, and peel and slice the onion.

Grease an ovenproof dish and alternate potatoes, onions, cured fish, and chopped dill.

Pour cream and milk in the pan and bake the pudding in the oven at 350°F (175°C) for about 40 minutes, until potatoes are thoroughly soft and pudding has a nice golden-brown color. If it is brown but the potato still feels hard, cover the pan with foil to prevent it from burning.

BROILED MUSSELS WITH GARLIC AND PARSLEY

Clean mussels, if necessary. Chop the onion finely and fry in a little oil in a wide saucepan. Add the mussels to the pan and pour the water and wine over them. Put the lid on and cook until the mussels have opened, about 5 minutes.

Strain the liquid and save it in the freezer to use for sauce for another time. (If you want to save it, feel free to add more vegetables such as carrots, fennel, garlic, and celery root.)

Remove one side of the shell from the mussels and place the half-shelled mussels in an ovenproof dish.

Chop the garlic and parsley finely and grate the cheese.

Spread the garlic, parsley, and cheese evenly over the mussels and broil them in the oven at 400°F (200°C) for about 5 minutes.

1 bag mussels (preferably Swedish-organic)
1 shallot
1½ cups (300 ml) white wine
1½ cups (300 ml) water
3 cloves garlic
1 bunch parsley
3.5 oz (100 g) Västerbotten cheese

MEAT

Knowledge through generations

In the Swedish peasant society, no food was thrown away in vain. Everything that was edible on an animal was used. Much of the time, the farmer sold the better parts like the chops and filet mignon to more affluent families. What was left, pieces for stew and offal, they used for themselves, and this was the beginning of traditional Swedish home-style cooking. From the head they made head cheese, the prime rib became casserole, from the blood they made black pudding or blood dumplings, the bones made a rich stock, the liver was saved for fancy parties, and anything else would be used for sausages that were hung to dry next to the stove.

In Lotten Lagerstedt's *Kokbok för skolkök och enkla hem* (*Cookbook for Home Economics Classes and Simpler Homes*), there are pictures of ox, pig, and veal with cutting charts, and below the images there are instructions on how to use the meat. Below the chart of a pig you find the text "1. The head is smoked, salted, or is used fresh to make headcheese. 2a. The fatback is salted or cut fresh and used for sausages or sandwich meats. 3b. The Spare ribs should be cooked fresh, till well done. 3. The rack of chops should be cooked fresh for chops." The list continues to number 10 where Lagerstedt writes that the feet can be cooked to make head cheese.

The refrigerator was invented in 1923 and did not reach the common man out in the country until a few decades later. Before the existence of the refrigerator, an important skill was passed down between generations, namely, how different parts of the meat should look and smell and how to store them in the best way. Today, the big food chains manage this for us with the date indicating the date of slaughter, packing, and "best before." The latter is often confused with an expiration date but should be seen just as a guideline.

To purchase meat of the best quality or determine the condition of the meat that we have already bought, we need to make use of our old skills. Different kinds of meat should not look alike, but what they all have in common is a dry surface and a fresh scent. Pork should be pink or pink and brown, beef anywhere between bright or deep red, and in marbled beef the fat should have a white or yellow color. Both veal and lamb should have firm white fat, but veal should have a slight pink tone while the lamb should be pink to dark pink.

Swedes love meat! They especially love the filet. This is very noticeable on restaurant menus: as a Swedish chef, when you have a dish with a filet on your menu, you know that the majority of the guests will choose that particular dish. I sometimes avoid putting filet mignon on the menu for just that reason, so that other dishes will not be forgotten.

I think it's a bit sad that many people do not use more of the animal and eat a larger variety of cuts. Often this is only because of a lack of knowledge of how to take advantage of a roast or shank. The easiest way to try out new parts is by talking to a butcher. In the Södermalm Food Hall, where I often shop, I usually ask the butchers for advice, to tell me what is in season, and how to cook a particular cut. In the past, I always went to the butcher to buy the most expensive cuts, but while traveling in the Basque country I was taught that the best purchases at the butcher are the cheaper parts of the animal, those that the supermarket chains throw away or grind down to ground meat.

Cutting chart beef

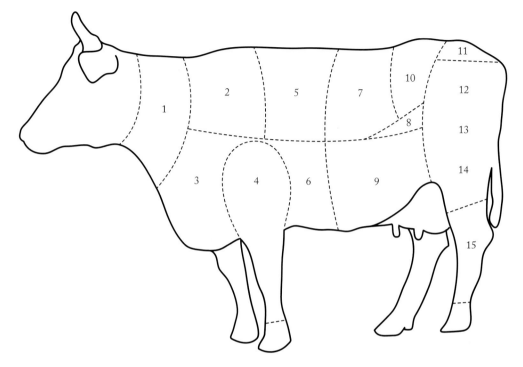

1. NECK
Suitable for ox cheek (see page 112) and other slow cooked dishes.

2. CHUCK
Perfect for slow-cooked dishes, such as beef stew on page 103.

3. FORE SHANK
Great for stews and other slow cooked dishes.

4. SHIN
Hard to get ahold of but suitable for confit and stews.

5. RIB
Can be grilled or roasted.

6. BRISKET
Available salted or fresh.

Cook it as on page 104. (Salt-cured beef brisket)

7. SHORT LOIN AND SIRLOIN
Sold with or without fat. Perfect for Sailor's beef on page 106.

8. FILET MIGNON
Cut the fillet of beef into small cubes and make Raw beef from the recipe on page 109.

9. FLANK
Usually goes in the grinder to make ground beef, for meatballs for example on page 125.

10. RUMP
Cook my roast beef on page 107.

11. TOP SIDE
Brown it and then roast it whole in the oven, or use it in Sailor's beef (see page 106).

12. TOP ROUND
Excellent for Steak tartar (see page 109) but preferably as ground beef.

13. SIRLOIN ROAST
This cut benefits from braising.

14. BOTTOM ROUND
Good to roast in the oven as roast beef on page 107.

15. SHIN
Good for stews and other slow-cooked dishes, but not easy to come by.

Cutting chart pig

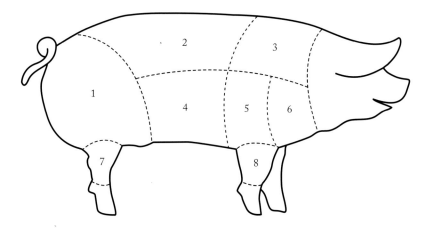

1. HAM
Make ham with cream sauce on page 116.

2. CHOPS AND SIRLOIN
Great for Rib roast on page 111 or for Pork schnitzel on page 118.

3. LOIN
Great to slice and barbecue, or roasted whole.

4. SIDE
Bacon is made out of the pork side, but also try the Pork side confit on page 117.

5. SPARE RIBS
Ribs can be purchased as thin or thick, and they should be slow-cooked or baked in the oven.

6. PICNIC SHOULDER
Is often bought salt-cured, and is great cooked and served with mashed turnips see page 167.

7. HAM HOCK
The front ham hock are larger and can be cooked as ham hocks on page 115.

8. HAM HOCK
Smaller ham hocks that are well-suited to serve one per person.

BEEF WITH HORSERADISH

1¾ lbs (800 g) of prime rib

STOCK
4 carrots
2 onions
2 bay leaves
1 large piece of horseradish
water
salt
*6 whole white peppercorns in
cheesecloth or a tea strainer*

SAUCE
*2 cups (500 ml) stock from
cooking the meat*
1½ cups (300 ml) cream
a dash of white wine vinegar
salt, if needed

FOR SERVING
Grated horseradish

Peel the onion, horseradish, and carrots, and put them along with the meat in a large saucepan. Bring to a boil and skim off carefully.

Lower the heat and cook slowly. Lift out the whole carrots and onions after about 15 minutes and continue to cook the meat for about 2 hours.

Take the meat out and let it rest in a warm place in the kitchen.

Measure 1¾ cups (400 ml) of the stock and let it reduce until about ⅔ is left, add the cream and cook for another 10 minutes. Season with salt and vinegar.

Cut the meat into slices, cut the carrots and onion into rough pieces. Serve with horseradish sauce, grated horseradish, and boiled mealy potatoes.

SWEDISH BEEF STEW (KALOPS)

Salt, pepper, and fry the chunks of meat in a hot pan with a little oil, let them brown properly and do not put too much meat in the pan at once.

Peel the onions and cut into rough chunks. Scrub the carrots if needed. Add the peppercorns in a tea strainer or in a piece of cheese cloth and tie it up.

Add meat, onion, whole carrots and spices in a large pot and cover everything with water.

Bring to a good boil and skim the pot carefully.

Reduce heat and continue boiling until meat is tender, about 2–3 hours.

Strain the liquid and let it reduce until ⅔ remains. Season the sauce with salt, pepper and beet juice.

Cut the carrots that cooked with the stew into smaller pieces and add them along with the meat in the pot. Remove the cheesecloth or tea strainer with the whole peppercorns. Heat everything up at a low temperature.

Serve the stew with boiled potatoes and pickled beets.

1¾ lbs (800 g) chunks of beef for stew
3 yellow onions
5 carrots
4 bay leaves
3 allspice kernels
4 black peppercorns
1–1½ cups (200–300 ml) liquid from pickled beets
water
salt, freshly ground black pepper

SALT-CURED BEEF BRISKET

CURING
1¾ lbs (800 g) beef brisket
4 cups (1000 ml) water
½ cup (100 ml) salt
2 bay leaves
5 white peppercorns

BRINE FOR COOKING IN
3 yellow onions
3 carrots
water

Salt-cured beef brisket is a true classic that tastes best with mashed turnips. You can make it out of already-salted meat or salt it yourself. If you buy salted meat, you can skip directly to step four in the recipe.

Boil the water for the brine in a saucepan and add salt and spices. Chill the brine.

Put the meat in a bowl that is only slightly larger than the meat and that can be sealed.

Pour the brine over the meat and leave the brine in the refrigerator for two days. Then take it out and discard the brine.

Put the meat in a large saucepan. Peel the onions and carrots and cut them into rough chunks. Add water to cover meat generously. Avoid salt as the meat is already salted.

Bring to a heavy boil and skim off carefully.

Continue to boil for at least 2 hours until meat is tender, but not falling apart.

Lift the meat out and place it on a baking sheet lined with parchment paper, cover with another parchment paper and another baking sheet, and refrigerate with a milk carton or something similar as a weight for a light press on the top sheet. Save the cooking liquid to be used for sauce or to cook mashed turnips from.

When the meat has cooled off, slice it into about ⅕ inch- (5 mm-) thick slices across the fibers, place on a baking pan, pour in a little of the stock from cooking, and heat with foil on top in the oven at 250°F (120°C) for 7–10 minutes. Serve with mashed turnips.

SAILOR'S BEEF

1¾ lbs (800 g) sirloin or short loin
1.1 lb (500 g) potatoes
3 onions
2 bottles of beer, preferably India Pale Ale
3 thyme sprigs
salt and freshly ground black pepper

Preheat the oven to 285°F (140°C).

Slice the meat in ⅕ inch (5 mm) slices, and peel and slice the onion the same way. Cut the potatoes into slices.

Season the meat and fry the slices in a hot pan with a little oil.

Layer the meat, potatoes, onions, and thyme sprigs on each other in an ovenproof dish with a lid or a clay pot, add salt and pepper in between the layers.

Pour the beer over and if necessary add water to cover.

Put the lid on and bake until the sailor's beef is done. It takes about 40 minutes to an hour. Check the potatoes occasionally. They should be soft but not falling apart.

ROAST BEEF À LA NIKLAS

Season the roast beef all around and brown it in a hot pan with oil. It must be evenly browned on all sides.

Put the meat on a baking sheet or in an ovenproof dish.

Roast it in the oven at 250°F (120°C) to an internal temperature of 155°F (68°C).

Serve the roast beef with potato salad, or with vegetables cooked with butter.

1 roast beef
salt and pepper
oil for cooking

ROAST BEEF "A roast beef cooked the English way should be 6–8 days old, during which time it's hung in a cold room and dried off daily. It is fried on a skewer over charcoal fire, which which is rarely done because requires great skill while cooking. The roast beef is wrapped in buttered paper, the skewer pierced right trough, and absolutely no spice is used. It is only cooked about a third of the way, so that it is still red inside and the meat within only slightly warm. It is then put in a roasting pan, covered with coarse salt to retain the juice, and allowed to stand in a hot oven for 30–45 minutes. Then it is removed and freed from salt and placed on the platter, which is usually garnished with vegetables, fried potatoes, etc. The dish is served with horseradish and braised onions. That English mustard is served goes without saying."—From *Modärn Kokbok* (*Modern Cookbook*), on roast beef the English way.

73. Steak tartare

STEAK TARTARE

Steak tartare can be varied end-lessly, but here is the recipe that I serve at Restaurang 1900, *which is very popular. It can be served as an appetizer with about 3.5 oz (100 g) or as main course with about 5.5 oz (160 g).*

Trim the meat and cut it with a sharp knife into small cubes. Chop the onion finely and combine with egg yolks only.

Salt and pepper the meat, and mix with remaining ingredients. Form the patty using a metal forming ring. Weigh it if you are uncertain.

Garnish with pickled beets, capers, parsley and shaved horseradish.

*14–22 oz (400–640 g) meat
   from the head and tail of a
   filet mignon
1 shallot
2 tablespoons Skåne mustard
4 egg yolks
4 tbsp cold-pressed rapeseed oil
salt and freshly ground black
   pepper*

FOR SERVING
*capers
pickled beets
horseradish
parsley*

BEEF À LA WALLENBERG

1.1 lb (500 g) minced veal
1¼ cup (400 ml) cream
1 egg yolk
finely ground white pepper
1 tablespoon (15 g) salt

FOR FRYING
1½ cups (300 ml) breadcrumbs
butter and oil

This is a truly classic dish that most people love, but which some believe is a bit difficult to prepare. It need not be if you prepare and weigh it carefully.

Measure out all ingredients and leave them in a cold place.

Take out a food processor and put the bowl in the freezer for about 15 minutes.

Take everything out and start to mix salt, white pepper, and minced veal. Pour the cream in a thin stream while constantly mixing until the ground veal absorbs all the cream. Add the egg yolk.

Shape round patties of ground meat at about 5.5 oz (160 g), and cover them with breadcrumbs.

Fry the Wallenberg patties in oil and plenty of butter. Place them on a baking sheet or ovenproof dish and cook in the oven at 250°F (120°C) to an internal temperature of 155°F (68°C).

Serve the patties with mashed or puréed potatoes, peas, lingonberries, and browned butter.

PORK LOIN WITH APPLES AND SUGAR-COOKED POTATOES

This roast is perhaps more Danish than Swedish, but is very popular in Skåne. Some make it with the pork side, but at Restaurang 1900, *we always make it with the loin and the fat cap attached. This steak with its crispy coat with syrup and apples is really good!*

Slit the fat cap along the pork loin, season with salt and pepper and brown thoroughly all around in a pan. It is important that the coat is crispy.

Put the meat in an ovenproof dish and drizzle syrup on top.

Bake in the oven till the roast is done at an internal temperature of 155°F (68°C).

Meanwhile, peel and cut potatoes into rough chunks, and cut the apples into wedges. Cook the potatoes in plenty of butter and oil. As the potato is starting to get some color and begins to turn brown, sprinkle with sugar and salt. Let it caramelize and add the apple wedges.

Slice the roast, pour the juices from the pan into a saucepan and give them a proper boil. Pour the liquid over the roast and serve with the fried potatoes and apple wedges.

PORK LOIN

1¾ lbs (800 g) pork loin, center cut with a thick rind or fat cap, skin intact
4 tbsp golden syrup
salt and freshly ground black pepper

POTATOES

1.3 lbs (600 g) waxy potatoes
butter and oil to cook in
sugar
salt

APPLES

4 tart Swedish apples

OX CHEEKS

2 ox cheeks
8 cups (2 liters) red wine for marinade
3 carrots
2 onions
2 sprigs of thyme
oil to fry in
water
salt and freshly ground black pepper
3 tablespoons sugar
8 cups (2 liters) red wine sauce
sherry vinegar
a dab of butter

Trim the ox cheeks from silver skin; the thicker, darker silver skin are boiled till soft, and therefore need not be trimmed away. Place the cheeks in a bowl, cover the meat with wine and wrap or seal the bowl and allow to soak in the fridge overnight.

Take out the bowl, strain off the wine and wipe off the ox cheeks with a towel or strong paper towels, and season with salt and pepper all over.

Heat a skillet on the stove and add a little oil. Brown the cheeks thoroughly all around and put them in a wide saucepan.

Peel and cut onions and carrots into rough pieces and add them to the pan. Add the water and the thyme.

Set the pan on the stove and let it come to a heavy boil, skim off carefully and then lower the temperature. Let it cook until the meat is really tender, which will take at least two hours.

Take out the cheeks, and strain the liquid through a fine sieve.

Place a saucepan on the stove and add the sugar. Add the strained liquid and the wine and let it reduce until half remains. Season the sauce with vinegar, salt, and freshly ground black pepper, and a dab of butter if needed. Slice and heat the ox cheeks in the sauce and serve them with puréed potatoes.

76. Ox cheeks

HAM HOCKS

Cut the vegetables into rough chunks and place in a saucepan along with the ham hocks and spices, cover with water.

Bring to a boil quickly, and skim off waste products that will move to the surface with a ladle.

Reduce temperature and cook for about 2 hours on low temperature. The meat will begin to come off the bone.

Remove the ham hocks from the pot, save the brine and use it for mashed turnips.

Serve the meat in a pot on the table, let everyone cut from the bones to serve themselves along with mashed turnips and mustard.

2 ham hocks
2 onions
3 carrots
2 bay leaves
5 allspice kernels

HAM WITH CREAM SAUCE

1¾ lbs – 2.2 lbs (800 g–1 kg) ham
salt and freshly ground black
pepper
oil for cooking

SAUCE
2 cups (500 ml) stock
1 onion
1 carrot
1 parsnip
1 cup (400 ml) cream
1 tablespoon jelly
salt and freshly ground black
pepper
a dash of white wine vinegar

Season the roast all over and brown it in a hot pan with a little oil. Bake in the oven till done to an inner temperature of 155°F (68°C). Remove the roast and let it rest in a warm place in the kitchen.

Peel and cut vegetables into coarse pieces, and fry them in a little oil in a large saucepan. Add the stock and let it all reduce until ⅔ remains.

Add the cream and cook for another 10 minutes. Season the sauce with salt, jelly, pepper, and vinegar.

Slice the steak thinly and serve it with boiled potatoes and applesauce or jelly.

PORK BELLY CONFIT

This is a dish that has been immensely popular in restaurants in recent years, but has by no means established itself as a home-cooked dish. Maybe many people believe that it is too complicated to cook, but it absolutely is not. It just takes some time, just about 4 days. But the result is worth the wait, and you can do what you want in the meantime.

Boil the water with the spices, then add salt. Chill properly. Place the pork belly in a deep container or jar that can be sealed. Pour the cold brine of the pork belly, make sure it is covered, and if needed add a small plate as a weight. Let the meat cure in a refrigerator for two days.

DAY THREE: Take out the lard and let it reach room temperature, set the oven temperature to 175°F (80°C) or slightly less than 212°F (100°C) if you have an older oven that cannot be set to precise degrees. Take the pork belly out of the salt brine and wipe it lightly with paper towel or a kitchen towel. Pour out the liquid, and place the meat in an ovenproof pan with high sides, or possibly in a clay pot. Add the lard and set the whole thing in the oven. After a while, when the lard has melted, place something ovenproof with a little weight on it on the top of the pork belly so that it's covered properly. Confit the pork belly in the fat overnight, about 10 hours.

DAY FOUR: Take out the meat and put it in between two baking sheets to press it. Place in the fridge.

FOR SERVING: Heat the oven to 300°F (150°C) degrees. Make serving pieces of approximately 5.5 oz (160 g), slitting the fat lightly and putting the pieces in an ovenproof dish with water in it. Leave in the oven for 12–15 minutes, until the fat is crisp and the meat is hot. Take the pieces of meat out of the water, and serve them with lacto-fermented cabbage.

1 pork belly, approximately 1¾ lbs (800 g)
6 cups (1500 ml) water
¾ cup (150 ml) salt
2 bay leaves
5 allspice kernels
3 thyme sprigs
4.4 lbs (2 kg) lard

PORK SCHNITZEL WITH HAM AND CHEESE

4 slices pork loin
8 slices aged cheese
4 slices good quality smoked
ham, such as Väddö ham
salt and freshly ground black
pepper

BREADING
1 scant cup (200 ml) flour
2 eggs
1 scant cup (200 ml) breadcrumbs

You can ask the butcher to pound the meat slices for you if you want. Use pork tenderloin or boneless pork chops.

Place meat slices on a clean counter surface, season with salt and pepper, and add cheese, ham and again cheese on each piece of meat.

Then fold them together and dip them first in flour, then lightly beaten egg, and finally in breadcrumbs.

Cook them in a hot frying pan with plenty of oil and butter.

80. Pork schnitzel with ham and cheese

81. Bacon-wrapped meatloaf

MEAT GRINDER *In the mid–1800s, the meat grinder was introduced. Previously, ground beef had been made with a time-consuming process with special so-called chopping knives. As the work took a very long time, few families has ground beef, apart from those with several maids who could do this for them. But thanks to the new invention, even common people could grind their meat into ground beef and create dishes such as meatballs, patties, stuffed cabbage, and sausage pudding. With a sausage-stuffer attached to the meat grinder, people could stuff sausage faster and more easily.*

BACON-WRAPPED MEATLOAF

Chop the onion finely and cook it till soft in a little oil without letting it get any color, then let it cool.

Soaked the breadcrumbs in milk and let thicken for a while. Combine all ingredients except bacon to a smooth mixture.

Prepare a clean counter surface by dragging a wet paper towel or a clean cloth across, so that the surface is slightly moist. Cover it with plastic wrap, about 16x16 inches (40x40 cm). Place bacon strips wrapped on top of each other on the plastic wrap and then place the ground meat in the middle on top of the bacon.

Roll up the whole thing with the plastic wrap into a round meat loaf, and twist the edges of the plastic wrap so that it is secure.

Bake at 175°F (80°C) loaf in the oven to an internal temperature of 155°F (68°C). Let the meatloaf cool slightly before removing the plastic and cut into thick slices.

1.1 lb (500 g) ground beef
1 yellow onion
1 scant cup (200 ml) milk
3 tablespoons breadcrumbs
1 egg
salt (about 1 tablespoon) (15 g)
freshly ground black pepper
2 packages of bacon

GAME PÂTÉ

9 oz (250 g) ground moose or elk
3–4 oz (20 g) egg white (from about ½ egg)
1 scant cup (200 ml) cream
½ tablespoon (7 g) salt

5 oz (150 g) of pig liver
3.5 oz (100 g) fatback
½ tablespoon (7 g) salt
1 egg

1 yellow onion
5 oz (150 g) funnel chanterelles
oil to fry in
9 oz (250 g) venison
1¾ oz (50g) thick cut bacon, cured

SPICE MIX
10 allspice kernels
10 green peppercorns
1 star anise
20 juniper berries
10 cloves
leaves from 5 sprigs thyme
2 tablespoons brandy
4 tablespoons port wine

This recipe is a for a loaf pan, but the pâté can also be baked in small individual molds.

Weigh all the ingredients in separate bowls or a mixing bowls and make sure they keep the same temperature, preferably refrigerated.

Chop the onions and the chanterelles, fry them in a hot frying pan in a little oil. Chill.

Dice the venison and the bacon in ½ inch (1 centimeter) sized cubes, and chill.

Mix the spices and the thyme leaves in a spice grinder or use a mortar and pestle.

Place the ground moose in a food processor along with salt and blend for about 30 seconds, then add the egg white and then the cream in a thin stream while mixing, until you have a fluffy basic batter. Place in a large mixing bowl and chill.

Place pig liver, fat, and salt in the food processor, and blend in the same way as the eggs and cream. Take out of the mixer and chill.

Take out all ingredients and fold them together with a spatula. Start by folding in the liver mixture into the basic batter, then add spices, onions, venison and bacon, and finish with cognac and port.

Fill a loaf pan with the mixture and bake in the oven at 250°F (120°C) to an internal temperature of 158°F (70°C).

Let the pâté cool in the pan, then chill it completely in the refrigerator, and take it out and place on a cutting board before serving.

GRANDMOTHER'S LIVER PÂTÉ

Weigh all the ingredients in separate bowls and set them out.

Chop the onion finely and dice the anchovies into fine pieces and chill.

Mix spices in a spice blender or use a mortar and pestle.

Dice the fatback finely, combine it with the liver and salt in a food processor and then mix for about 30 seconds.

Add the egg and cream in a thin stream and blend until all the cream is absorbed into the batter.

Put the mixture in a large mixing bowl and fold in the herbs, anchovy fillets and onions.

Fill the mixture into ovenproof dishes that holds about ¾ cup (150 ml), but fill them only to ⅔.

Bake in the oven at 250°F (120°C) to an internal temperature of 158°F (70°C).

350 g veal liver
7 oz (200 g) fatback
½ tablespoon (7 g) salt
1 egg
¾ cup (150 ml) cream

1 inch dried ginger
2 cloves
5 white peppercorns
5 anchovy fillets
½ yellow onion

84. Meatballs with cream sauce

MEATBALLS WITH CREAM SAUCE

Peel the onion and mix with a little cream in a food processor. Mix the rest of the cream and milk with the onion mixture, spices and breadcrumbs into a paste.

Add the ground beef and mix thoroughly by hand or in mixer, but be careful, the batter should not start to form filaments, which will make the meatballs hard and tough.

Roll the meatballs in desired size and place them on an oiled baking sheet. Bake them in the oven at 212°F (100°C), with a bit of steam if you have that feature in your oven, otherwise you can pour very little water on the baking sheet. The meatballs should get firm, squeeze them with two fingers, and if they do not feel loose inside, they are ready. It takes about 10 minutes.

Then fry the meatballs in plenty of butter and oil. Serve themwith mashed or puréed potatoes, cream sauce, lingonberries, and pickled cucumber.

CREAM SAUCE: Peel and chop the onion and fry in a large pan with a little oil. Chop the anchovy and add it.

Add the veal stock and let it reduce until about ⅔ remains. Add the cream and cook another 10–15 minutes.

Thicken with a little cornstarch blended with a bit of water, and season with pickle juice from the cucumbers and liquid from the lingonberries, salt, and pepper. Mix lightly with an immersion blender and strain the sauce through a fine sieve. Taste and season again.

Serve the sauce with the meatballs, meat patties, or meatloaf.

2.2 lbs (1 kg) ground beef
½ onion
½ cup (100 ml) milk
¾ cup (150 ml) cream
salt (about 1 tablespoon) (15 g)
1 tsp ground allspice
½ cup (100 ml) bread crumbs

CREAM SAUCE
1 yellow onion
1 anchovy fillet
4 cups (1000 ml) veal stock
4 cups (1000 ml) cream
corn starch
a little liquid from the pickled cucumbers and the lingonberry sauce
salt and freshly ground black pepper

STUFFED CABBAGE ROLLS

1 large head of cabbage

MEAT MIXTURE
51.1 lb (500 g) ground beef
1 onion
1 scant cup (200 ml) cooked long grain rice
½ cup (100 ml) cream
salt and freshly ground black pepper
golden syrup

Scoop out as much as possible from the stem of the cabbage without breaking the leaves, then boil the cabbage in a large pot of generously-salted water. Pick off the leaves as they begin to fall off. It helps if you, have a large slotted spoon to lift the cabbage with. Place the cabbage leaves between kitchen towels or sturdy paper towels.

Chop the onion finely or grate it on a grater. Mix it with the rest of the ingredients for the batter.

Place each cabbage leaf on a clean counter surface and use a small paring knife to remove the roughest part of the leaf. Shape small "sausages" of the batter and put them in the cabbage leaves. Fold in the ends of each leaf and then roll them together. Place them on an oiled baking tray with the seam down.

Drizzle plenty of syrup on the rolls and bake them in the oven at 400°F (200°C) for about 5 minutes. Then lower the temperature and continue to bake until the ground meat has reached an internal temperature of 155°F (68°C). Serve the stuffed cabbage with boiled potatoes, lingonberry jam and pickled cucumber, and cream sauce, if desired.

STUFFED CABBAGE ROLLS These ground beef cabbage rolls have their roots in the Turkish dish *dolmasi* where the word *dolma* means "filling." Neither the Turks nor the Swedes are alone in making this dish. In fact, it comes in several variations in both Central and Eastern Europe. It is believed that the stuffed cabbage reached the Swedes when the Turks with their families arrived there during Karl the 12th's reign, and settled down in order to try to get back the money they had lent to the king. During this time, the Turkish women told the Swedish women of their dish *dolmasi,* and the Swedish in turn made their own version of it, stuffed cabbage. The first time we encounter this dish written down is in Cajsa Warg's cookbook from 1756.

85. Stuffed cabbage rolls

86. Chicken liver pâté

CHICKEN LIVER PÂTÉ

Weigh all the ingredients in separate bowls and make sure they are cold.

Melt the butter in a saucepan, then take the pan off the heat and let cool to as close as possible to room temperature, pour the melted butter into another container, being careful not to include the white milk protein.

Chop the shallots finely and cook along with port wine over low heat until half remains. Refrigerate.

Dice the anchovies finely. Add liver, salt, the port and shallot reduction, garlic, and anchovies in a food processor and blend till smooth.

Add butter in a steady stream. Season with pepper.

Fill the mixture into ovenproof dishes that hold about ¾ cup (150 ml), but fill them only to two-thirds.

Bake the pâtés in the oven at 195°F (90°C) in the oven until the batter is firm. Test by shaking the pan a little. It should look like a crème brulée or omelet that just firmed up.

Cool the pâtés and allow to stand in a cool place a few hours before serving.

14 oz (400 g) butter
1 shallot
1¾ cup (400 ml) port wine
2 anchovy fillets
14 oz (400 g) chicken livers
½ tablespoon (7 g) salt
1 small garlic clove
freshly ground black pepper

CHICKEN SAUSAGE

1.1 lb (500 g) ground chicken
1 container casings
2 cups (500 ml) cream
1 tablespoon salt
1 shallot, finely chopped
⅓ ounce (5 g) fat back, finely minced
2 tablespoons Skåne mustard
1 bunch parsley, chopped
2 tablespoons chicken stock
4 teaspoons (20 ml) white port wine
4 teaspoons (20 ml) Madeira
freshly ground black pepper
bay leaf
butter and oil to fry in

Weigh all ingredients and set them cold. Rinse the casings in cold water for 20 minutes to remove the salt brine that they are in when you buy them.

Take out a food processor and a large mixing bowl and place in freezer for a while.

Mix the ground chicken with salt in the food processor and add the cream in a thin stream.

Put everything in the large bowl and mix the batter together, add the liquid last.

Slip the casing on a sausage stuffer, and tie a knot in the end. Make sure you have water nearby, if the casing becomes dry it cracks easily.

Add the batter into the stuffer, cranking out the mixture with one hand and holding the casing with the other to ensure that no air bubbles form; turn the casing when you get a sausage the size you want.

Boil a pan of water, salt, and the bay leaf and add the sausages, then pull the pan from the heat and let sausages slowly simmer till done. If the sausages are not to be served immediately they should be cooled down as soon as possible.

FOR SERVING: Fry the sausage in plenty of oil and butter.

LAMB LIVER SAUSAGE

Rinse casing in cold water for 20 minutes to remove the salt that they are in when you buy them.

Chop the onion and apple finely and fry them in a pan with some oil, without browning. Refrigerate.

Mix the lamb liver with the fat back, salt, and pepper, and chill.

Mash the boiled potatoes and mix with onion and apple. Then mix everything by hand and add the spices.

Slip on the casing on the sausage stuffer, and tie a knot at the end.

Make sure you have water nearby, if the casing becomes dry it cracks easily.

Add the batter into the stuffer, cranking out the mixture with one hand and holding the casing with the other to ensure that no air bubbles form; twist the casing when you get a sausage the size you want.

Boil a pan of water, salt, and the bay leaf and add the sausages, then pull the pan from the heat and let the sausages slowly simmer till done. If the sausages are not to be served immediately they should be cooled down as soon as possible.

When serving, fry the sausage in plenty of oil and butter.

1.1 lb (500 g) lamb liver
1 container of hog or lamb casing
1.1 lb (500 g) minced fatback
salt and freshly ground white pepper
1 yellow onion
1 apple
3 boiled potatoes
1 teaspoon ground cinnamon
1 teaspoon ground coriander seeds
½ cup (100 ml) water
bay leaf
butter and oil to fry in

VEAL SAUSAGE

1.1 lb (500 g) of double ground veal
1 container casings
1.1 lb (500 g) double ground pork (Ask for twice ground at the butcher's)
7 oz (200 g) minced or finely diced fat back
2 pinches ground green pepper
1 teaspoon salt
¾ cup (150 ml) veal stock
1 heaping cup (250 ml) water
¼ cup (50 ml) cognac

Making sausage at home is not as difficult as you might think—a little messy maybe, but if you start out with a clean and tidy workplace it is completely straightforward. If you don't have a sausage stuffer, you can put the batter in a piping bag with a wide tip and pipe the batter into the casing. However, it may be easier if you do this with another person, so that one person is in charge of the casing and twists the sausage, while the other cranks or fills with the bag.

Rinse the casing in cold water for 20 minutes to remove the salt that they are in when you buy them.

Make sure all ingredients are cold, mix everything except the liquid by hand or in a food processor.

Add the liquid slowly. Put the batter in the fridge, put the casing on the sausage stuffer and tie a knot at the end of it.

Make sure you have water nearby, do not let the casings dry out. Put the batter into the sausage stuffer and crank it out. Spin the casing in between each sausage, at the size you prefer.

Save 4 inches (10 cm) of casing at each end. Simmer sausages in salted water to an internal temperature of 149°F (65°C). If the sausages are not going to be served immediately, they should be chilled as quickly as possible. When serving: Fry the sausages in butter and oil.

VEAL SAUSAGE Even though sausage was eaten at Gustav Vasa's court, it has always been considered very simple food in Sweden. In the 1800s, it was mostly laborers who ate sausages, and the sausage makers were largely single women who took advantage of the waste parts from the slaughterhouses and made sausages with spices.

89. Veal sausage

CHICKEN CURRY *You might think that chicken with curry sauce is something that came to Sweden in the 1970s, when the dish was in its heyday, but curry has been in Sweden for much longer than that. I have found recipes for chicken in curry from the early 1900s.*

We had a lot of exotic spices in Sweden earlier than people might think; they were imported by various tradesmen and early explorers. But during the two world wars everything became scarce, and there was some struggle before exotic spices could make a comeback.

One could whether chicken in curry sauce should be considered classic home cooking, but if Hagdahl says so, then I agree. Either way and above all, the dish is very good.

CHICKEN CURRY

Coarsely chop the chicken so that you get two breasts, two thighs and two wings, save the carcass in the freezer to make the stock with later.

Season the chicken with curry powder, cayenne pepper, salt, and black pepper, and cook in a cast iron pan on the skin side and all around.

Chop the onion, carrot, and apple finely and add it to the pan, let it brown slightly.

Add the water and bring to a boil. Skim off carefully and put a lid on the pan, lower the heat and continue to cook slowly for 40 minutes to 1 hour or until the meat starts to separate from the bones. The time depends on size of the chicken, because it increases the cooking time from a technical standpoint but also because larger, older chickens have longer, coarser fibers will be tastier if they cook a little longer.

Remove the chicken and let it cool slightly, then pick the meat from the bones and set it aside.

Let the sauce reduce until half remains, then add the cream and cook for another 10 minutes. Mix the sauce and then strain it. Add the chicken to the pan and heat over low heat.

Serve the stew with steamed rice.

1 whole organic chicken
2 onions
2 carrots
2 tart apples
salt and freshly ground black pepper
1–2 tbsp yellow curry, depending on quality
1–2 pinches of cayenne pepper
water
1¾ cup (400 ml) cream

91. Chicken liver

INTESTINE *Viscera intestines from slaughtered animals were called* pölsemat *or minced meat. When people used up the more exlusive cuts, just the* pölsemat *remained and was made into sausages. The final remains were boiled together with barley and made into a hash that was eaten the days following the slaughter.*

CHICKEN LIVER

Clean the liver from all skins and tendons.

Cut the bacon into rough cubes and chop the onion finely.

Fry the bacon until it has browned and released a lot of the fat.

Add the chicken liver and onions and let them cook with the bacon. Season with salt and pepper.

Serve right out of the pan with parsley and croutons.

14 oz (400g) chicken livers
3.5 oz (100g) thick cut bacon
1 yellow onion
croutons
parsley
salt and pepper
oil

LAMB IN DILL SAUCE

1¼ lbs (800 g) pieces of lamb
for stew
1 onion
1 carrot
1 bunch dill
1 tablespoon dill seeds
3 teaspoons salt
1¾ cup (400 ml) cream
½ cup (100 ml) vinegar
¼ cup (50 ml) sugar
freshly ground white pepper

Peel the onion and carrot and cut into rough chunks. Pick the tops of the dill, chop them, and save the stems for the sauce.

Place onion, carrot, pieces of lamb, and dill in a saucepan. Tie the dill stalks with cooking twine and add them as well. Cover all with water and season with salt.

Let come to a heavy boil and skim off. Then lower the temperature and cook for about 1 hour until the meat becomes tender.

Take the meat and dill stalks out, put the meat on the side and discard dill stalks.

Add cream to the sauce. Reduce the sauce until about ⅔ remains.

Season the sauce with sugar, vinegar, and freshly ground white pepper.

Return the meat to the pan and add the chopped dill. When the meat is hot, serve with boiled potatoes.

92. *Lamb in dill sauce*

93. *Leg of lamb with parsley*

LEG OF LAMB WITH PARSLEY

In Husmoderns kokbok (The Housewife's Cookbook) *there is a recipe for parsley-stuffed lamb roast, where the roast is stuffed with parsley butter, and browned and cooked slowly until the juices then turn into a creamy sauce. Here is a recipe inspired by that one, but without the cream and butter. A little healthier, but just as good!*

Mix parsley, garlic, and oil. Season the roast with plenty of salt and pepper, and rub in half of the parsley mixture into the meat.

Bake in the oven at 285°F (140°C) to an internal temperature of 150°F (67°C), for 1½–2 hours.

Serve the roast with the rest of the herb oil as a cold sauce. The roast can be eaten either hot or cold, preferably on a buffet or at a family dinner, where someone will cut the slices as you eat.

1 leg of lamb on the bone
1 bunch parsley
1 clove garlic
¼ cup (50 ml) oil
salt and pepper

VEGETABLES

Raw vegetables — out of style

"The difference between a rich man's and a peasant's table appears rarely in something as plain as the dish of vegetables, they may originally have been as equally good in one place or the other, but their taste and appearance differs completely for better or worse depending on the preparation."

— Ch. Em. Hagdahl

Before modern supermarkets were filled with products all year round, people depended on filling their own pantries with food for the long eight months of winter without fresh produce. The rich families that could fill their shelves to the brim held very high status. This created a trend in which it was believed that it wasn't healthy to eat vegetables and root vegetables raw, so instead everything was cooked for a long time. The longer they were boiled, the better, and therefore families also let the soup or stew space too big hang in the three-legged cauldron over the fire and simmer for several hours.

Root vegetables that are cultivated in Swedish soil are of high quality. There are few plants that can grow in the Nordic climate, but those that can develop an extra intense flavor under the strong sun of the summer months. In Sweden, root vegetables have filled up many hungry stomachs throughout time with their high content of vitamins, carbohydrates, minerals, and fiber. Moreover, it is very easy to cook edible roots and vegetables and they provide plenty of flavors.

"That the root crop, called the potato, is one of the best gifts nature bestowed upon mankind, can not be disputed."

When potatoes reached Sweden in the 1600s, many were very skeptical of the almost tasteless root. But when the severe crop failure came in 1772, the Swedes discovered how good the rugged and versatile tuber was: it both filled you up and made an excellent aquavit. The name in Swedish, *potatis*, was imported by Jonas Ahlströmer himself and came from the English word potatoes. Today, a smorgasbord with herring would seem incomplete without new summer potatoes. Christmas dinner would miss it's Jansson's Temptation, and meatballs with cream sauce would miss their boiled potatoes.

Swedish home cooking is not known for plates and dishes filled to the brim with fresh vegetables, which it is not surprising given the history of our crops and climate. Nowadays, when we have vegetables all year round, it is difficult to understand what it was like to only have potatoes, onions, root vegetables, and cabbage, if that, during much of the year. But when you read and consider old recipes, you understand where the term "meat and potatoes" comes from. Tubers of various kinds have played a major role in our survival, and I think most Swedes would agree with me when I say that potatoes are absolutely delicious!

In my home-style cooking, I would like to keep these traditions and avoid exotic imported plants and leaves, or other newcomers in the produce section. I would rather use of what we have in season in Sweden, and even if those vegetables and tubers are also imported all year round, I would much rather use the Swedish-grown vegetables when they are at their best. With a little planning, you can also take advantage of the seasonal vegetables available to you: parboil and freeze or dry mushrooms, and store tubers and onions in a dark, cool place. Vegetables with plenty of chlorophyll, such as spinach and broad beans, are great to freeze.

POTATO *Perhaps the most widely-used crop in Swedish home-style cooking is the potato, which has been grown here for a long time. It tolerates our climate and comes in many different varieties. You can vary its preparation tremendously, but the recipe should be adapted to the variety of potato. Mash made out of waxy potatoes gets tougher because it contains more starch, and mealy potatoes must be cooked very gently so they do fall apart and become watery.*

MASHED POTATOES

1.3 lbs (600 g) mealy potatoes
salt
1¼ cup (400 ml) milk
5 oz (150 g) butter

Take out the butter and let it reach room temperature. Peel the potatoes and place in a saucepan, cover them with water and season with salt.

Let the water come to a boil and then lower the heat to a little over medium. Keep cooking until a knife can easily be removed from the potato. Meanwhile, heat up the milk.

Discard the potato water and let the potatoes steam off properly. Mash the potatoes with a potato masher and add hot milk and butter. Season with salt and serve with meatballs, meatloaf, or seared salmon.

OVEN-ROASTED POTATOES

For roasted potatoes, most often I use a waxy variety, but mealy varieties work as well. The potatoes become soft in the center and require a little less time in the oven. They should be roasted skin side down in the pan so that they don't stick.

Preheat the oven to 440°F (225°C).

Wash the potatoes thoroughly, and scrub them with a scrubbing glove or sponge if they are really dirty. Cut the potatoes into desired shape with a paring knife.

Place the potatoes on a baking sheet with the cut edges turned up so that they will roast properly. Roast the potatoes in the oven with oil, butter, and salt, and set the timer for 10 minutes to start with. Turn the baking sheet around if your oven cooks unevenly, and shake the baking sheet to roast evenly.

When the potatoes have a golden-brown color, they should be done, but check with a fork, and lower the heat and roast them longer if they are still hard.

1.3 lbs (600 g) potatoes of your choice
salt
oil or butter

CREAMED POTATOES

1.3 lbs (600 g) waxy potatoes
salt

CREAM SAUCE
2½ cups (600 ml) milk
1 knob of butter
3 tablespoons flour
salt
freshly ground white pepper
nutmeg
1 bunch dill or parsley or
a generous amount of Skåne
mustard

Wash the potatoes thoroughly and cut them into smaller pieces.

Put them in a large pot and add enough water to just cover them. Season with salt and put on the stove. Let the water come to a boil and then lower the heat to about medium. Keep boiling until the potatoes release easily from a paring knife.

Boil the milk, melt butter in another saucepan and add flour. Whisk it so that the flour combines well with the butter. Add the hot milk while constantly whisking.

Continue to cook the sauce for another 15 minutes on very low heat, and whisk thoroughly so the stew does not burn on the bottom. Season the sauce with salt, grated nutmeg, and freshly ground white pepper.

Chop the herbs and stir them in, or season with mustard, then add the boiled potatoes.

Serve the stewed potatoes with veal sausage, salt cured, or seared salmon.

POTATO PURÉE

Take out the butter and let it reach room temperature. Peel the potatoes and boil gently in salted water until they release easily from a small paring knife.

Peel and cut onion into rough pieces, and cook together with white pepper and milk.

When the potatoes are done, drain and allow to steam properly. Mash them in a potato ricer. Strain the milk, add the butter to the pressed potatoes, and stir with a whisk. Add the milk and stir some more.

1.3 lbs (600 g) mealy potatoes,
  like Swedish peanut fingerling
salt
1¾ cup (400 ml) milk
7 oz (200 g) butter
4 white peppercorns
1 shallot

98. Potato pancakes

POTATO PANCAKES

Grate the potatoes coarsely and lightly salt them. Let sit for a while and then squeeze out the liquid formed by the salt on the potatoes.

Heat a frying pan, add oil and butter, and add a thin layer of grated and washed potatoes in the pan. Press them slightly with a spatula. Reduce the heat on the burner and let the potatoes fry till crispy, about 3 minutes. Then flip and cook for another 10 minutes.

Use multiple pans to get all the pancakes finished at the same time, or heat the oven to just below 212°F (100°C) and let the finished potato pancakes rest there until all are ready to be served.

Serve them as a side with fish or meat, as a little appetizer with bleak roe and sour cream, or with something salty and sweet such as sweet fried thick-cut bacon and lingonberries.

14 oz (400 g) of any mealy potato variety, but not as mealy as the Swedish peanut fingerling potato
salt
butter and oil to fry in

POTATOES AU GRATIN

1.3 lbs (600 g) potatoes of a medium waxy kind
1½ cup (300 ml) milk
1½ cup (300 ml) whipping cream
2 cloves garlic
black pepper
salt
7 oz (200 g) grated cheese, preferably Västerbotten
a knob of butter

There are few things more certain than that everyone loves potatoes au gratin! From time to time it has been very popular to serve this potato dish, both at home and in restaurants. Unfortunately, you always have to scrub the oven after you make a gratin . . .

Here is a recipe that makes it easier to avoid the burnt mess by parboiling potatoes with cream and milk. This recipe also makes it easier to serve the potatoes in individual portion forms, if desired.

Peel and slice the potatoes.

Press or chop the garlic and use a mortar and pestle to mix it with a handful of black pepper.

Take a large saucepan and an ovenproof dish that holds at least 8 cups (2 liters) or a bunch of ramekins or other small ovenproof dishes, and turn the oven to 400°F (200°C).

Add potatoes and garlic to the pan and pour in the cream and milk, add salt and cook on low heat in the milk and cream until the potatoes are almost finished. This will take about 30 minutes.

Stir occasionally, and season with black pepper and more salt if needed.

Grease the pan with some butter and fill it with creamed cooked potatoes. Sprinkle with cheese and bake the gratin until it has a nice golden-brown color. Bake 10–15 minutes.

POTATO SALAD WITH SKÅNE MUSTARD AND DILL

Wash the potatoes thoroughly and cut them into smaller pieces. Place in a large saucepan and cover with water, add salt and boil the water, then lower the temperature and continue to boil over low heat until potatoes easily release from a small paring knife. Discard the water and let the potatoes cool to at least room temperature.

Mix egg yolks with the mustard and vinegar in a bowl with a whisk or in a mixer. Season with salt and add oil in a thin stream while constantly whisking. Continue until you have a thick mayonnaise. Sometimes you don't need all the oil, and sometimes you need more. It is also a matter of how thick you want the mayo. Chop the dill and mix it with the potatoes in the mustard mayonnaise.

Serve the potato salad at a buffet or as a side dish with salt-cured salmon. You can also add onions or other vegetables, or change the herbs to taste.

1.3 lbs (600 g) of a waxy potato

VINAIGRETTE
3 egg yolks
¼ cup (50 ml) Skåne mustard
1 dab hot mustard
3 tablespoons white wine vinegar
salt
about 8 oz neutral oil
1 bunch dill

CABBAGE *Cabbage is the Swedish equivalent of leafy greens and the nearest to lettuce you can get. It is not very easy to grow, as many animals like it as well. But it is hardier than lettuce leaves and has a much longer shelf life. The Swedish have always used it, both as a side dish, or supplement more expensive raw materials. .*

SOUR CABBAGE

½ head green pointy cabbage
1 teaspoon salt
2 tablespoons white wine vinegar
chopped herbs

Slice the cabbage as thinly as possible. Put it in a plastic bag with salt and vinegar and let sit overnight.

Then press out excess liquid and serve the cabbage as a salad with herbs, or as a side dish with sausages.

101. Sour cabbage

SWEDISH GREEN CABBAGE

2.2 lbs (1 kg) kale
½ cup (100 ml) any stock,
chicken is great, but vegetable
stock also works well
1½ cups (300 ml) cream
1 knob of butter
salt and freshly ground white
pepper
light syrup
vinegar

This is a dish often served at Christmas dinner, and is most popular in the Halland region of Sweden. It's almost like a stew, but if you want a slightly lighter dish you can exclude the cream and reduce the amount of butter; however some kind of fat is needed, so a good oil is always tasty.

Pick the cabbage off the stems and shred them. Boil plenty of salted water and blanch the cabbage quickly. Let it drain thoroughly in a colander.

Then fry the cabbage in a wide frying pan or cast iron pot over medium heat with butter and syrup.

Pour the stock over and cook for about 10 minutes on low heat, then add the cream and cook for a little longer.

Season the cabbage with salt, peppar, and vinegar, and possibly some more syrup.

RED CABBAGE

Shred the cabbage finely, and cut the apples into wedges and the onion into thin rings. Fry them in oil in a large saucepan. Place all spices in cheesecloth or a tea strainer.

Add spices, syrup, vinegar, butter, and possibly a little water to cover the cabbage.

Cover with a lid and lower the heat, let the cabbage cook slowly under the lid and stir occasionally. Add some more water if the cabbage is still hard, and the liquid has evaporated. Season with salt and pepper.

*½ red cabbage, about 1.1 lb
   (500 g)*
2 tart Swedish apples
1 onion
oil for frying
1 cinnamon stick
2 bay leaves
1 star anise
3 whole cloves
1 knob of butter
*¼ cup (50 ml) red wine
   vinegar*
4 tablespoons syrup
*salt and freshly ground black
   pepper*

CREAMED VEGETABLES *Many vegetables in Swedish home-style cooking are served creamed and personally I think this style of preparation tastes really good. Below are my favorite recipes for creamed vegetables. Frozen blanched vegetables works well for these recipes, especially for green vegetables, since they keep the best and retain the most flavor in frozen form. I make two different sauces, which I then add to different vegetables or flavor differently: a béchamel (white sauce with milk in it) or a double cream (cream reduced to half).*

CREAMED CABBAGE

½ head cabbage

SAUCE
2½ cups (600 ml) cream
white wine vinegar
salt and a pinch of sugar

Cut away the core of the cabbage and cut the rest into large chunks. Heat the cream in a saucepan and let it reduce until about ⅔ remains.

Fry the cabbage in a hot frying pan with oil and sprinkle with salt and sugar and a dash of vinegar. When the cabbage has softened slightly and is shiny, transfer it to the saucepan with the cream and cook for another 10 minutes. Serve the cabbage as a side dish with sausage or meat.

CREAMED SPINACH

Pick the spinach leaves off the stems, wash them thoroughly. Boil plenty of salted water and blanch the spinach quickly. Leave to drain in a colander.

Boil the milk and cream; this helps to prevent the sauce from burning on the bottom.

Let the butter melt in another saucepan and add the flour. Whisk it carefully and add warm milk and cream, whisking constantly. Continue to cook the sauce for another 15 minutes, making sure that it does not burn on the bottom. Season the sauce with freshly ground white pepper, nutmeg, and salt.

Stir in the spinach, and heat it in the sauce. Serve the creamed spinach as a side dish, for example with white fish.

1 large bunch spinach (about 10.5 oz (300g)

SAUCE
1½ cups (300 ml) milk
½ cup (100 ml) cream
1 knob of butter
2 tablespoons flour
freshly ground white pepper
salt
nutmeg

CREAMED SALSIFY

1 bundle salsify

SAUCE
vinegar
juice and grated zest from
½ lemon
2.5 cups (600 ml) cream
salt

Heat a saucepan with plenty of salted water.

Fill up a bowl with water, add vinegar and lemon juice. Peel the salsify under running water and cut off any bad parts. Put them in the acidified water as soon as you finish as they oxidize and darken very quickly when exposed to air.

Meanwhile, pour the cream in a pan and let it cook on the stove over low heat until half remains.

Cut the salsify to the size that you like and place in the saucepan with boiling water. Boil them for about 3 minutes, until tender, but let them still have a little hardness in the core. Drain and let the salsify steam off properly.

Then combine them with the cream and season the sauce with grated lemon zest and salt.

CREAMED FAVA BEANS

Fava beans are delicious, even if they are a bit hard to shell. First, they must be removed from the pod, and then they must be shelled before you get to the actual bean. They can also be purchased frozen, and then you only have to remove the shell.

Heat a saucepan with plenty of salted water. Pour the cream in another pan and let it reduce slowly on the stove until half remains.

Blanch the beans for about 4 minutes in salted water, then pour off the water quickly. Cool them in cold running water so they don't overcook.

Then remove the skins that are bitter and tough.

Mix the beans with the cream and season with salt, nutmeg, and freshly ground white pepper.

14 oz (400 g) fava beans, removed from their pods

SAUCE
*2½ cups (600 ml) cream
salt
freshly ground white pepper
nutmeg*

CREAMED CARROTS

6 carrots

SAUCE
1½ cups (300 ml) milk
½ cup (100 ml) cream
1 knob of butter
2 tablespoons flour
freshly ground white pepper
salt
nutmeg

Peel and cut carrots into coins. Heat a saucepan with plenty of salted water and blanch the carrots for about 2 minutes. Strain the water and let the carrots steam properly.

Boil the milk and cream; this helps to prevent the sauce from burning on the bottom.

Let the butter melt in another saucepan and add flour.

Whisk it carefully to avoid lumps and add the warm milk and cream while constantly whisking. Continue to cook the sauce for another 15 minutes, making sure that it does not burn at the bottom.

Season the sauce with freshly ground white pepper, nutmeg, and salt, and mix it with the carrots. Serve as a side dish with sausage.

CREAMED JERUSALEM ARTICHOKES

Heat a saucepan with plenty of salted water. Add cream and wine in another saucepan and let it reduce until half remains.

Peel and cut the Jerusalem artichokes in half with a paring knife. Rinse in cold water to remove soil and any peel that might be left. Blanch them in the water for 4–5 minutes, depending on the size of the pieces that you have. Strain the water and let the artichokes steam properly.

Mix them with the cream and season with salt and pepper.

Cut the chives finely and add, if you like.

1.1 lb (500 g) Jerusalem artichokes

SAUCE
2½ cups (600 ml) cream
½ cup (100 ml) white wine
salt and freshly ground black pepper
1 bunch chives, optional

JERUSALEM ARTICHOKE PURÉE

1.1 lb (500 g) Jerusalem artichokes
oil
1 shallot
2 cloves garlic
1½ cups (300 ml) white wine
1½ cups (300 ml) cream
salt and freshly ground black pepper

Preheat the oven to 480°F (250°C).

Scrub the artichokes thoroughly with a wire brush, scrubbing mitt, or sponge. Cut them in half or into three parts if they are large.

Place them on a baking sheet and drizzle oil over them, season with salt, and roast in the oven for about 10 minutes until they have a nice golden-brown color.

Peel and chop the onion and garlic coarsely, place in a large saucepan together with the artichokes and add the wine.

Let the wine reduce and add the cream. Let this reduce too but not completely. Mix the purée in a food processor or with an immersion blender, though in this case the food processor is more efficient and provides a smoother cream. Season with salt and pepper.

GREEN PEAS WITH BUTTER

Green peas lose very little color, flavor, and nutrition when they are frozen, and they are really good as they are, just thawed. But if you heat them with a little onion, butter, and herbs, they will be great. This side dish is a must with Beef à la Wallenberg.

Chop the shallots and parsley finely, and melt a knob of butter in a saucepan.

Add the peas and onions in the butter, and cover with water. Warm lightly, and boil until the first bubble appears.

Add chopped parsley, season with salt, and serve the peas immediately.

14 oz (400 g) green peas
1 shallot
1 knob of butter
a pinch of salt
water
1 bunch parsley

112. Celeriac purée

CELERIAC PURÉE

Preheat the oven to 440°F (225°C). Peel and cut celeriac into rough pieces and place them on an oiled baking sheet. Season with salt and roast in the oven for about 10 minutes until they turn golden-brown.

Place the roasted celeriac in a saucepan, put on the stove, and add the wine.

Let the wine reduce and add the cream. Let it also reduce but not completely. Season with salt and pepper.

Blend to a smooth purée in a food processor. Serve as a side dish on a buffet with croutons, or even with meat or sausage.

1 celeriac
oil
1 scant cup (200 ml) white wine
1½ cups (300 ml) cream
salt
freshly ground black pepper

MASHED TURNIPS

Peel and cut the vegetables into equally sized pieces. Put them in a saucepan, add stock, cover up with water if needed, and boil. Then lower the heat and continue cooking over low heat until the vegetables release easily from a small paring knife.

Pour off the liquid and let the roots steam properly. Mash them with a potato masher and add the butter. Season with salt.

Serve the mash with ham hocks or salt-cured beef brisket.

2 carrots
1 small turnip
4 mealy potatoes
½ celeriac
4 cups (1000 ml) stock from pork or salted beef brisket
7 oz (200 g) butter
salt

ROASTED JERUSALEM ARTICHOKES

1.1 lb (500 g) Jerusalem
artichokes
salt
oil

Preheat the oven to 440°F (225°C).

Scrub the Jerusalem artichokes thoroughly with a wire brush, scrubbing mitt, or sponge. Cut them in half or into three parts if they are large.

Put them on a baking sheet and drizzle with oil. Season with salt and roast in the oven for about 15 minutes until they get a nice golden-brown color and are soft but not mushy in the middle.

ROASTED CHESTNUTS

1.3 lbs (600 g) chestnuts
coarse salt

Preheat the oven to 440°F (225°C).

Dry chestnuts on a rough kitchen towel and make a ½ inch (1 ½ cm) deep cross in the chestnuts' pointed ends. Put

them in a frying pan, on a thick layer of coarse salt.

Roast them for about 20 minutes and serve with stirred butter, as a side dish or as a small appetizer.

114. Roasted Jerusalem artichokes

DESSERTS & BAKED GOODS

The wood stove paved the way for cookies

In the middle of the 1800s, something great happened in the history of kitchens: the wood stove was introduced in Sweden. Before then the Swedish had fried donuts, fattigman cookies, and rosettes in boiling hot oil, extended an iron with a long wooden handle to bake gingerbread over the fire, and baked bread in outside ovens. People in the country were skeptical towards the new invention, because it took away the working light generated by the fireplace, but in town it was received with open arms because it required less of the expensive firewood. When ovens were installed under the wood stoves, baking became even easier.

A little later, cookies and coffee parties were introduced into Swedish homes. The coffee break now known as a *fika* was unique to Sweden and was named *kafferep* (coffee ripping), which is presumed to derive from the fact that the parties were not just about drinking coffee, but also involved ripping up silk swatches for padding clothes. Nowhere else did people serve coffee, coffee cake, and cookies like they did in Sweden. The concept of "seven kinds of cookies" originates from the 19th century etiquette rules that said that at least seven varieties of cookies should appear on the cookie platters. The more cookies on the platter, the higher the creative homemaker's status and the greater the attention from their sweets-craving girlfriends. For ease, cookie recipes derived from a basic dough recipe of flour, sugar, butter, egg yolks, and water.

Since Alice Tegner's songbook *Sjung med oss, Mamma (Sing With Us, Mom)* came out in 1892, Swedes have been singing the children's song *En sockerbagare (A Pastry Chef)* around Christmas. In Germany, the word *sockerbagare* was the term for the people that made cast-sugar tops, but when the word came to Sweden it became a term for someone who baked sweet pastries, marzipan, and chocolates. In the 1800s that professional title was changed to *konditor (pastry chef)*, a word which derived from the French *condire* meaning, "to make tasty." The *pâtisserie* became a meeting place where women could meet without their husbands and be served. At the more exclusive establishments, they could even get a little fortified wine with the pastries.

Desserts really differed from other sweets. The term did not include baked goods or ice cream but marmalades, fine pastries, compotes, and puddings that were all served hot or cold. These were called *entremets*, meaning in-between courses—what we today call desserts.

172

When I started culinary school at the age of 16, I was more interested in riding around on my skateboard and drinking beer with my friends than in cooking, and dessert for me then was a big tub of ice cream with chocolate fudge eaten while watching music videos on TV. One day when I asked my cooking teacher what kind of sweets we were making in class, I got reprimanded in a way that I will never forget.

"Niklas, when you're at home watching TV you eat sweets, but at a restaurant you eat dessert!"

This has always stayed in my mind. Sweets are something simple that you can eat after dinner, a piece of cheese or pie. At a restaurant chefs try harder and work longer to make a dessert. On the following pages you will find no desserts. Instead you will find my sweets. Things that I like to eat at the end of a meal without the need for tempering chocolate or making cotton candy. Good luck!

117. Vanilla custard

SOUFFLÉ *The base of a soufflé is always a flavored cream with cornstarch in it, such as vanilla custard. You can use this recipe and replace the flavorings for the taste you want in your soufflé.*

VANILLA CUSTARD

Boil the milk and vanilla. Let sit for at least 20 minutes. Whisk the egg yolk, sugar, and cornstarch till fluffy. Add the milk and return to the stove. Cook for another 5 minutes under constant heavy whisking. Add the butter and whisk it into the cream.

Strain the custard into a fine mesh strainer, and chill it.

WHEN SERVING: Dilute the custard with lightly whipped cream, crème fraiche, or milk, depending on how you will use it. The custard cream can be frozen and taken out later, so it does not matter that this recipe makes quite a lot.

2 cups (500 ml) milk
1 vanilla pod
4 oz (120 g) egg yolks
⅔ cup (125 g) sugar
¼ cup (30 g) cornstarch
2 tablespoons (25 g) unsalted butter

VANILLA SOUFFLÉ

4 tablespoons vanilla custard
4 egg yolks
8 egg whites
1 pinch salt
1 tablespoon sugar

Preheat the oven to 355°F (180°C)

Take out two wide clean bowls, a spatula, and a whisk. Break the egg whites in one bowl and the yolks in the other. Add the vanilla custard to the yolks and stir carefully with a spatula.

Beat the whites vigorously until a foam is formed, add sugar and salt and continue beating until egg whites are fluffy and creamy.

Gently fold egg whites into the cream and yolk mixture in three batches and without taking too much air out of it.

Grease four ovenproof ramekins that hold at least ¾ cup (150 ml) and coat them thoroughly with sugar. Pour the batter into the ramekins and bake in the oven for 7–10 minutes, until soufflé has risen and has a golden-brown color on top.

117. Vanilla soufflé

RHUBARB SOUFFLÉ

4 tablespoons of the vanilla custard made from the vanilla custard recipe on page 175 but with rhubarb juice/purée instead of milk (also, use a little less sugar because the purée and juice already have sugar in them)
4 egg yolks
8 egg whites
1 pinch salt
1 tablespoon sugar

Preheat the oven to 355°F (180°C).

Take out two wide clean bowls, a spatula, and a whisk. Break the egg whites in one bowl and the yolks in the other. Add the vanilla custard to the yolks and stir carefully with a spatula.

Beat the whites vigorously until a foam is formed, add sugar and salt and continue beating until egg whites are fluffy and creamy.

Gently fold egg whites into the cream and yolk mixture in three batches and without taking too much air out of it.

Grease four ovenproof ramekins that can hold at least ¾ cup (150 ml) and coat them thoroughly with sugar. Pour the batter into the ramekins and bake in the oven for 7–10 minutes, until soufflé has risen and has a golden-brown color on top.

APPLE SOUFFLÉ

Preheat the oven to 355°F (180°C).

Take out two wide clean bowls, a spatula, and a whisk. Break the egg whites in one bowl and the yolks in the other. Add the vanilla custard the the yolks and stir carefully with a spatula.

Beat the whites vigorously until a foam is formed, add sugar and salt and continue beating until egg whites are fluffy and creamy.

Gently fold egg whites into the cream and yolk mixture in three batches and without taking too much air out of it.

Grease four ovenproof ramekins that can hold at least ¾ cup (150 ml) and coat them thoroughly with sugar. Pour the batter into the ramekins and bake in the oven for 7–10 minutes, until soufflé has risen and has a golden-brown color on top.

4 tablespoons of the vanilla custard made from the recipe on page 175 but use apple juice instead of milk
4 egg yolks
8 egg whites
1 pinch salt
1 tablespoon sugar

PISTACHIO SOUFFLÉ

4 tablespoons vanilla custard from the recipe on page 175 but with 4 tablespoons pistachio paste for additional flavoring (available in well-stocked grocery stores or in French bakeries, similar to Odense soft nougat but made out of pistachios)
4 egg yolks
8 egg whites
a pinch of salt
1 tablespoon sugar

Take out two wide clean bowls, a spatula, and a whisk. Break the egg whites in one bowl and the yolks in the other. Add the vanilla custard to the yolks and stir carefully with a spatula.

Beat the whites vigorously until a foam is formed, add sugar and salt and continue beating until egg whites are fluffy and creamy.

Gently fold egg whites into the cream and yolk mixture in three batches and without the taking too much air out of it.

Grease four ovenproof ramekins that can hold at least 3⁄4 cup (150 ml) and coat them throoughly with sugar. Pour the batter into the ramekins and bake in the oven for 7–10 minutes, until soufflé has risen and has a golden-brown color on top.

LINGONBERRY PEARS

Boil the water and wine with spices and lingonberries. Add sugar and stir.

Peel the pears and place them in the syrup as you peel. Cover the pears with a parchment paper, so that all are covered with liquid.

Then boil the pears until they are soft enough to easily release from a paring knife.

Eat the pears immediately with whipped cream, or store them in a clean sealed container.

8 pears of a firm varietal
10.5 oz (300 g) lingonberries
1 scant cup (200 ml) sugar
1 scant cup (200 ml) red wine
1 scant cup (200 ml) water
1 cinnamon stick
2 star anise
1 vanilla pod

122 . *Raspberry compote*

123 . *Blueberry soup*

124 . *Rosehip soup*

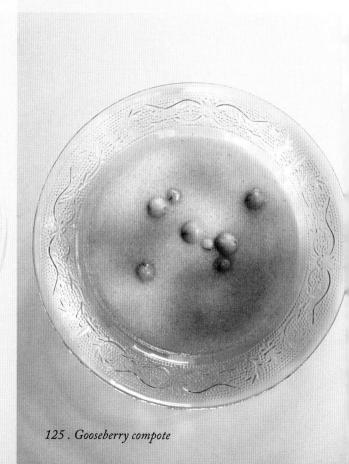

125 . *Gooseberry compote*

RASPBERRY COMPOTE

Cook berries, sugar, wine, and water for about 10 minutes. Blend with an immersion blender and strain carefully.

Bring to a boil again and thicken with potato starch according to the directions on the package.

2 cups (500 ml) frozen raspberries (or fresh if available)
1 scant cup (200 ml) sugar
1 scant cup (200 ml) white wine
water

BLUEBERRY SOUP

Mix all ingredients and cook over low heat for at least 20 minutes. Pour the soup into a fin-meshed sieve. Let the juice run through at its own pace, and do not force it.

Taste the soup and cook to reduce a little more if you like.

1.1 lb (500 g) blueberries
1½ cups (300 ml) white wine
1 scant cup (200 ml) sugar
1 vanilla pod
zest from ½ lemon
water, if needed to cover the berries

ROSEHIP SOUP

1 scant cup (200 ml) dried
rosehip peel
½ cup (100 ml) sugar
1 scant cup (200 ml) dry white
wine
2 cups (500 ml) water
honey
1 lemon, zest and juice
1 orange, zest and juice

Boil sugar, water, and wine, then add rose hips and citrus zest, lower the heat and continue boiling for about 10 minutes, and then turn off the burner. Let it sit for at least 10 minutes.

Blend with immersion blender and strain through a fine sieve, then season with honey and lemon juice. The soup will last at least a week in the fridge and can be heated or eaten cold, but may need to be diluted a bit if it's been a few days, as it tends to thicken.

GOOSEBERRY COMPOTE

2 cups (500 ml) frozen goose-
berries (or fresh if available)
1 scant cup (200 ml) sugar
1 scant cup (200 ml) white
wine
water
potato starch

Cook berries, sugar, wine, and water for about 10 minutes. Blend with an immersion blender and strain carefully.

Bring to a boil again and thicken with potato starch according to the directions on the package.

BLUEBERRY COMPOTE

Scrape out the seeds from the vanilla pod and cook it with berries and sugar over very low heat. Cook until the compote has a thick consistency. It takes about 15 minutes.

Serve the compote with ice cream or whipped cream, and perhaps sponge cake.

14 oz (400 g) blueberries
1 scant cup (200 ml) sugar
1 vanilla pod

CORDIAL SOUP

Boil the cordial and water.

Then mix with potato starch mixed with a little water. Bring to a boil again and whisk thoroughly, then taste the soup and season with juice from ½ lemon, dried fruit or citrus peel to taste.

2 scant cups (450 ml) berry cordial
6 cups (1500 ml) water
2 tablespoons potato starch
juice of ½ lemon
optional: dried fruit and candied lemon peel

CHEESECAKE

DAY 1, CHEESE CURD
8 cups (2 liters) milk
1 tablespoon flour
1 tablespoon liquid rennet

DAY 2, BATTER
4 eggs
1¾ cup (400 ml) cream
1 tablespoon flour
1 tablespoon sugar
2 grated bitter almonds
½ cup (100 ml) chopped almonds

DAY 1, CURD: Heat the milk in a saucepan to 98°F (37°C) and add flour and rennet. Let sit for about 20 minutes until it has set and has a creamy consistency.

Whisk a little bit and then pour the mixture into a sieve with cheesecloth or a kitchen towel in it.

Refrigerate overnight so that the curd and the whey separate. The curd is what is used for the cheesecake.

DAY 2, BATTER: Mix all ingredients for the batter, then add the cheese curd. Spread the batter into one large or several small ovenproof dishes. Bake in oven at 400°F (200°C) for about 5 minutes for small dishes and for about 15 minutes for larger.

If you double the recipe you might want to reduce the heat after a while so that the top doesn't get burnt while the middle is still runny. Serve the cheesecake with lightly whipped cream and jam.

KALVDANS (RAW MILK PANCAKE)

Preheat the oven to 350°F (175°C)°.

Dilute the colostrum with regular milk (otherwise the *Kalvdans* becomes too hard). How much milk to use depends on the "potency" of the colostrum. If it is the first milk right after the calf is born it will be extra potent and needs to be diluted a little more, if it's from the third day it's weaker and will not need to be diluted as much.

Cook a sample, perhaps in a cup that you put in a pot of water. If it sets it's fine, and if it is too hard it needs to be diluted with more milk; if it is too loose and does not set it needs more colostrum. Season the milk with salt, sugar, and cinnamon or cardamom.

Pour into a greased ovenproof form. Bake in the oven with the dishes in a double boiler setup for about 30 minutes. When the *Kalvdans* has set and has a beautiful color it is done.

Serve it right out of the pan with jam or compote. If you have a surplus of colostrum you may deep freeze it already diluted and flavored.

4 cups (1000 ml) diluted raw milk (colostrum + milk)
sugar
salt
cinnamon or cardamom

RAW MILK PANCAKE Kalvdans is made out of colostrum, which is the first milk from a cow after she has given birth. Colostrum has extra protein and fat for the calf to get a good amount of nutrition and grow properly. And that is exactly what gives the Kalvdans its special character. Kalvdans is traditionally seasoned with vanilla, cardamom, cinnamon, or saffron.

VANILLA CUSTARD SAUCE

1 vanilla pod
1 cup (250 ml) milk
1 cup (250 ml) cream
3 egg yolks
½ cup (100 g) sugar

Cut the vanilla pod, then scrape out the seeds and put them into a saucepan with the milk and cream. Bring to a boil and then let cool for about 5 minutes.

Whisk egg yolks with the sugar and add the milk and cream while constantly stirring. Heat until the sauce begins to thicken or until the first small bubble is visible, at about 185°F (85°C).

Cool the sauce directly and place it in the refrigerator for at least 1 hour or overnight so that it can mature.

COFFEE *Around 1710, Stockholm got its first coffee house, and by the middle of the century coffee houses were flourishing in most of Sweden's cities. These houses became gathering places, especially for politicians and the "intelligentsia," because these upstairs rooms were usually nicer than restaurants, which were often in basements. In 1855 there was a ban on home distilling, and in retaliation the peasant cast in the parliament made sure that there was also a coffee ban, which hit the coffeehouses hard. By the end of the 1800s coffee reached all of the people of Sweden, and coffee replaced alcohol as the drink of choice.*

CAKE *Originally even bread was labeled cake, but later the word came to have the meaning that it has today. From the 1600s we find gingerbread, rosettes, donuts, wafers, and communion wafers. All of these were called cakes.*

ALMOND WREATHS

Preheat the oven to 250°F (120°C).

Beat the egg whites until stiff. Mix in sugar and lemon zest.

Fill the mixture into a pastry bag and pipe wreaths on a greased baking sheet. Sprinkle with sugar and chopped almonds and bake the cookies until they have a light yellow color and are dry.

DOUGH
2 egg whites
1½ cups (150g) caster sugar
zest of ½ lemon
2 teaspoons granulated sugar

DECORATION
sugar
finely chopped almonds

FATTIGMAN COOKIES

DOUGH
3 egg yolks
1 scant cup (90g) caster sugar
4 tablespoons heavy cream
1 cup (125 g) flour
zest of ½ lemon

FRYING
2.2 lbs (1 kg) cooking oil or
coconut butter freshly ground
cinnamon and sugar

DAY 1: Whisk together the egg yolks and sugar. Whip the cream until stiff and mix it into the egg mixture along with lemon zest.

Sift the flour and mix well. Then cover the bowl with plastic wrap and let sit in the refrigerator till the next day.

DAY 2: Roll out dough ¼ inch (½ cm) thick. Cut strips, 1–1 ½ inches (3–4 cm) wide and 4–5 inches (10–12 cm) long. Make a slit in the middle of each strip, slip one end through the slit for the characteristic shape.

Heat the oil to about 320°F (160°C) in a cast iron pot or some other sturdy pot. Fry a few cookies at a time until they get a golden-brown color. Lift them with a slotted spoon and roll them in cinnamon and sugar while hot.

FATTIGMAN COOKIES The most common name for these in Sweden is *klenäter*, which is believed to have derived from the word *klenoder*, meaning treasures. This cookie is one of our oldest and dates back to the Middle Ages. Without a wood stove these were baked by cooking in hot oil, what we today call deep-frying. *Klenäter* are said to have been one of Gustav Vasa's favorites.

CINNAMON BUNS

Preheat the oven to 480°F (250°C).

Boil half the milk with the cardamom seeds and then pour it over the cold milk. Let sit for a while. Check the temperature, it should not be higher than 98°F (37°C).

Strain the cardamom seeds and crumble the yeast. Add the remaining ingredients and knead by hand or in a kitchen mixer. The dough should be soft and supple and release easily from the side of the bowl.

Allow the dough to rise for 30 minutes under a kitchen towel, and then take it out and divide it into four parts. Roll each portion into a ⅕ inch (5 mm) thick rectangle.

Mix sugar, butter and cinnamon and spread it on top of the dough.

Roll up the dough and cut them into about ½ inch (1½ cm) thick slices. Place each slice on a parchment paper and let rise under a kitchen towel for 10 minutes.

Beat the egg with a little water and brush on each bun. Sprinkle pearl sugar on top and bake the buns in the oven for about 15 minutes.

DOUGH
2 cups (500 ml) milk
2 oz (50 g) fresh yeast
5 oz (150 g) softened butter
1 teaspoon salt
1 tablespoon granulated sugar
10 cardamom seeds
2 lbs. (900 g) flour (about 5¾ cups (1400 ml))

FILLING
7 oz (200 g) butter, at room temperature
½ cup (100 ml) sugar
2 tablespoons freshly ground cinnamon

TOPPING
1 egg
pearl sugar

134. Jellyroll

JELLYROLL

Preheat the oven to 480°F (250°C).

Beat eggs and sugar until fluffy, preferably with an electric beater. Sift the flour and baking powder and mix gently. Add milk and mix everything to a smooth batter.

Spread the batter on parchment paper in a 12x16 inch (30x40cm) baking pan. Bake in the oven at 480°F (250°C) for 5 minutes. If you have a convection function on your oven bake it in the middle at 400°F (200°C)for 8 minutes and set it on hot air.

I think it's easier to get good results with a convection oven. If you use a regular oven please note that you really need to watch the cake for the last minute so that it does not burn.

Place the cake directly on parchment paper sprinkled with sugar. Pull off the paper that the cake was baked on. Spread immediately with filling and roll up. Let the jelly roll cool off seam down before cutting it into slices.

BATTER
3 eggs
1 scant cup (200 ml) granulated sugar
1 scant cup (200 ml) flour
2 teaspoons baking powder
¼ cup (50 ml) cream or milk

FILLING
1 scant cup (200 ml) solid raspberry jam

CURRANT CAKE

7 oz (200 g) butter
1 heaping cup (250 ml) sugar
2 eggs
1½ cups (300 ml) currants
½ cup (100 ml) golden raisins
grated zest of one lemon
⅜ cup (75 ml) milk
1¼ cups (400 ml) flour
1 pinch of baking powder

Preheat the oven to 300°F (150°C).

Beat sugar and butter and add the eggs one by one.

Soak the currants and the raisins for a little while. Mix flour and baking powder and add it to the butter, sugar, and egg mixture.

Strain the currants and raisins and add them with the lemon zest and milk.

Grease and flour a loaf pan and pour the batter into it. Bake in the center of the oven for about 1½ hour.

SPONGE CAKE

Grease and flour an angel food cake pan, slightly larger than 1½ quarts (1½ liters). Preheat the oven to 350°F (175°C).

Beat eggs and sugar until white and fluffy with an electric mixer. Sift flour, vanilla, sugar, and baking powder into the egg mixture and fold carefully until you have a smooth batter.

Melt butter, add the water and bring to a boil. Then pour it into the batter and whisk until smooth.

Once the batter is smooth pour it into the cake pan and place directly into the oven. It is important to be fast because the heat makes the baking powder react.

Bake in the bottom of the oven for about 45 minutes. Let the cake cool in the pan for a little while. Remove from pan and turn upside down. Let the cake cool with the pan over it.

3 eggs
1½ cups (300 ml) granulated sugar
2 teaspoons vanilla
2 teaspoons baking powder
2.5 oz (75 g) margarine or butter
½ cup (100 ml) water
1½ cups (300 ml) flour

137. *Blueberry pie with oatmeal crumble*

BLUEBERRY PIE WITH OATMEAL CRUMBLE

Cut the butter into cubes and mix it with flour, sugar and oats. Fill an ovenproof dish with the butter and sprinkle sugar over the blueberries.

Spread the crumble over the pie and bake in the oven at 400°F (200°C) for 15 minutes.

1.1 lb (500 g) blueberries
½ cup (100 g) sugar

DOUGH
7 oz (200 g) butter
1 scant cup (200 ml) rolled oats
1 scant cup (200 ml) flour
½ cup (100 ml) sugar

RHUBARB PIE WITH CARAMEL CARDAMOM CRUMBLE

Cut the rhubarb into pieces about ½ inch (1 cm) thick. (If the skin is rough, you may need to peel them.) Sauté them with sugar for about 4 minutes. Place them in an ovenproof pan.

Cut the butter into cubes and mix with remaining ingredients into a dough. Spoon out the dough over the rhubarb and bake in the oven at 355°F (180°C) for 15 minutes.

14 oz (400 g) rhubarb
¼ cup (50 ml) sugar

DOUGH
7 oz (200 g) butter
1¾ cups (400 ml) flour
1 scant cup (200 ml) sugar
1 tablespoon ground cardamom

138. Rhubarb pie with caramel cardamom crumble

139. *Apple cake from Skåne*

140. Pear tart

APPLE CAKE FROM SKÅNE

Shred the pumpernickel with a cheese grater, or blend in a food processor. Fry the crumbs in plenty of butter with the sugar.

Layer the crumbs with apple-sauce in an ovenproof dish, and put dabs of butter on top. Bake in the oven at 355°F (180°C) for about 15 minutes.

1 sweet dark rye bread, such as pumpernickel
2 cups sugar
14 oz (400 g) butter
2 cups (500 ml) homemade applesauce

PEAR TART

Mix all ingredients for the dough in a bowl and place in the refrigerator for a while. Peel and slice the pears and sprinkle sugar over them.

Roll out the dough onto a clean and floured countertop. Line a pie pan with the dough and cut the edges off carefully. Prick the dough with a fork in the bottom of the pan and cover with a piece of parchment paper cut into a round shape, same size as the pan. Fill with peas or beans as a weight.

Bake in the oven for about 10 minutes at 355°F (180 C)°. Remove pie and fill it with the pear wedges. Sprinkle with more sugar and bake on 355°F (180°C) for about 20 minutes, or until the pears caramelize and have a nice color.

4 pears
¼ cup (50 ml) sugar

DOUGH
18 tablespoons (250 g) butter
1½ cups (600 ml) flour
4 tablespoons sugar
4 tablespoons water

14 oz (400 g) of dried peas or beans (to use as a weight for the crust)

ALMOND CAKE WITH CLOUDBERRIES

4.5 oz (130 g) egg
6 tablespoons (75 g) sugar
1 tablespoon (10 g) brown sugar
1.5 oz (45 g) flour
1.5 oz (45 grams) almond flour
1 teaspoon (5 g) baking powder
3 grated bitter almonds
6½ tablespoons (90 g) melted cooled butter

NO COOK CLOUDBERRY
JAM
10.5 oz (300 g) cloudberries
1½ tablespoons (20 g) granu-lated sugar
1½ tablespoons (20 g) brown sugar

Beat eggs, sugar, and brown sugar.

Sift the flour and baking powder. Mix with a spatula.

Fold in the butter and almonds.

Bake in a greased portion sized pan at 355°F (180°C) for 10 minutes until the cake has golden-brown color.

Place frozen or fresh berries with sugar in a bowl. Leave at room temperature and stir occasionally until the sugar has dissolved.

Serve with the almond cake.

If you have any leftovers, you can store them in an airtight glass jar in the fridge for at least a week.

141. Almond cake with cloudberries

PRESERVES

Keep the harvests of the seasons in jars

"Canned foods are prepared in such a way that they can stay fresh for a long time, despite the seasonal changes. Two methods are used for this."

—Charles E. Hagdahl

Originally the art of preserving was necessity, and about survival. In the summers people harvested the grains of the fields and milked the cows, and in the early fall the animals were slaughtered; and along the coasts, people fished. Everything was preserved to eat during the months until the next summer came with new crops, new milk, and fresh meat. The grains were used for cooking and baking, the milk was made into butter and cheese, the fish and meat were salted or smoked, the berries were dried or made into jams, and vegetables were pickled in vinegar. Preserving was simply the Swedes' way of taking care of spring', summer', and fall's harvests before the long, cold winter. Even today, preserving is an important part of our home cooking in dishes such as traditional pickled beets, lingonberry jam, and salted butter.

By preserving we prolong the durability of a food by preventing microorganisms from attacking it. This stops the natural decomposition process that would normally cause the raw food to rot, mold, ferment, or dry out. The most common preservation method was salt-curing, but since we don't have salt naturally in Sweden it had to be imported. And the farther north in the country, the more expensive the salt. Therefore, we developed a different preservation technique called fermentation, which is unique to Nordic countries. Fermentation is a technique, in which the decomposition is controlled, as seen in dishes like fermented herring and gravlax.

The traditional and historical preservation methods include drying, salt curing, smoking, parboiling, and canning in airtight jars. In more recent years we have also used refrigeration, freezing, heating, vacuum packing, and various different chemically-derived preservatives.

Classic Swedish fare does not use many vegetables. And those that are served are pickled. Before the advent of greenhouses, the vegetable season was extremely short. Vegetables were ripe for just a few weeks a year, and then had to be taken care of right away. People pickled, salted, and preserved as much as they could in order to have a good stock for the rest of the year. Nowadays you can get most vegetables all year round, and as a result our knowledge about preserving our own vegetables is disappearing slowly but surely. Therefore I think it is very important that we preserve our foods so that this knowledge isn't lost.

Preserved berries and vegetables are very well suited to Swedish dishes. The acidity in quick pickled cucumbers complements a dish of meatball, and the sweetness of the lingonberries with a meatloaf is fantastic.

142. Cloudberry cordial

143. Sour blueberry cordial

CLOUDBERRY CORDIAL

*2.2 lbs (1 kg) berries, frozen
are fine, but they should be as
ripe as possible
1½ cups (300 ml) water
2½ cups (600 ml) sugar per
4 cups (1 liter) drained juice
juice from 2 lemons*

Place cloudberries together with water in a saucepan, and allow to boil. Cook on low heat for about 10 minutes.

Strain the juice through a fine strainer and cheesecloth, and then measure the drained juice. Measure the sugar according to the amount of juice, and pour everything back into the saucepan, making sure that no pieces of berries remain.

Cook the juice again till the sugar melts, remove any foam, and add lemon juice. Pour the cordial into thoroughly cleaned bottles, preferably just cleaned and dried in the oven at 212°F (100°C) for about 5 minutes so that no water is left in them.

When serving, mix the cordial with cold water, about 1 part cordial to 4 parts water.

SOUR BLUEBERRY CORDIAL

Measure the berries and water and place in a well-cleaned saucepan, and boil thoroughly. Remove the foam that has formed, and let sit for a while.

Strain the cordial through a fine sieve and cheesecloth, and pour the well-drained cordial into thoroughly cleaned bottles, preferably just cleaned and dried in the oven at 212°F (100°C) for about 5 minutes so that no water is left in. Since this cordial contains no sugar, it won't keep as long as regular cordial and should be kept in the fridge.

4.4 lbs (2 kg) blueberries
2 cups (500 ml) water

144. Elderberry cordial

145. Raspberry cordial

ELDERBERRY CORDIAL

2.2 lbs (1 kg) elderflowers
16 cups (4 liters) water
8.8 lbs (4 kg) sugar
4 lemons
4 teaspoons citric acid

Make a simple syrup by boiling the water and sugar, stir the citric acid with a little water and mix it into the simple syrup.

Wash the lemons thoroughly, slice them thinly and place them in the bottom of a well-cleaned bucket. Place the flowers on top and pour the simple syrup over it. Cover with plastic wrap and let the bucket stand in a cool place for three days.

Strain the juice through a fine strainer and cheese cloth and pour the cordial into thoroughly cleaned bottles, preferably just cleaned and dried in the oven at 212°F (100°C) for about 5 minutes.

Mix 1 part of the cordial concentrate and 3 parts water.

RASPBERRY CORDIAL

Place raspberries with water in a saucepan, and let come to a boil. Cook on low heat for about 10 minutes.

Strain the cordial through a fine sieve and cheese cloth, and then measure up the strained cordial. Measure the right amount sugar by the amount of cordial, and pour everything back into the saucepan, making sure that no pieces of berries remains.

Boil the cordial again so the sugar melts, then remove any foam and add lemon juice. Pour the cordial into thoroughly cleaned bottles, preferably just cleaned and dried in the oven at 212°F (100°C) for about 5 minutes so that no water is left in them.

When serving, mix the cordial with cold water, about 1 part cordial to 4 parts water.

2.2 lbs (1 kg) raspberries, frozen are fine, but they should be as ripe as possible
1½ cups (300 ml) water
2½ cups (600 ml) sugar per 4 cups (1 liter) drained juice
juice of 2 lemons

RHUBARB CORDIAL

4.4 lbs (2 kg) rhubarb ripe rhubarb
1¼ cup (400 ml) water
2½ cups (600 ml) sugar per
4 cups (1 liter) strained juice
juice of 2 lemons

Wash the rhubarb well and cut into pieces and place in a well-cleansed saucepan with the water. Bring to a boil and cook over low heat for about 10 minutes

Strain the cordial through a fine sieve and cheesecloth, and then measure up the drained cordial. Measure the sugar by the amount of cordial, and pour everything back into the saucepan, making sure that no berries remain.

Cook the cordial again so the sugar melts, remove any foam, and add lemon juice. Pour the cordial into thoroughly cleaned bottles, preferably just cleaned and dried in the oven at 212°F (100°C) for about 5 minutes so that no water is left in them.

When serving, mix the cordial with cool water, about 1 part cordial to 4 parts water.

NO-COOK LINGONBERRY JAM

Place the berries in a bowl and mix them with sugar. Let the mixture stand at room temperature and stir with a spoon carefully cleaned from time to time.

Repeat this until the sugar has melted completely. It takes about 6 hours.

Keep the jam in sterilized jars in the refrigerator.

2.2 lbs (1 kg) frozen lingon berries
¾ cup (150 ml) granulated sugar
¾ cup (150 ml) brown sugar

LINGONBERRY JAM

Place the lingonberries and water in a saucepan and bring to a boil. Remove foam and add the sugar. Cook over low heat until the jam has a temperature of 225°F (107°C).

Test the jam by putting a little on a plate, if you can draw a line through it and it doesn't float back together again it is ready.

Pour the jam into clean glass jars and let cool. Seal the jars and store the jam in a cool place.

4 cups (1 liter) lingonberries
1 cup (250 ml) water
14 oz (400 g) sugar

148. *Lingonberry jam*
149. *The Queen's jam*
150. *Raspberry jam*

THE QUEEN'S JAM

Mix berries and sugar and leave out at room temperature until sugar has dissolved, which takes about 6 hours. Stir occasionally.

Cook the mixture in a very clean saucepan until the jam has a temperature of 225°F (107°C).

Test the jam by putting a little on a plate, if you can draw a line through it and it doesn't float back together again it is ready.

Pour the jam into clean glass jars and let cool. Seal the jars and store the jam in a cool place.

1.1 lb (500 g) raspberries
1.1 lb (500 g) blueberries
10.5 oz (300 g) sugar

RASPBERRY JAM

Mix berries and sugar and leave out at room temperature until sugar has dissolved, it takes about 6 hours. Stir occasionally.

Cook the mixture in a very clean saucepan until the jam has a temperature of 225°F (107°C).

Test the jam by putting a little on a plate, if you can draw a line through it and it doesn't float back together again it is ready.

Pour the jam into clean glass jars and let cool. Seal the jars and store the jam in a cool place.

2.2 lbs (1 kg) raspberries
10.5 oz (300g) sugar

STRAWBERRY MARMALADE

3.3 lbs (1.5 kg) strawberries
1¾ lbs (800 g) sugar

Rinse and clean the strawberries, then mix berries and sugar and leave out at room temperature until sugar has dissolved, which takes about 6 hours.

Heat up the mixture in a very clean saucepan until the marmalade has a temperature of 225°F (107°C).

Test the jam by putting a little on a plate, if you can draw a line through it and it doesn't float back together again it is ready.

Pour the marmalade into clean glass jars and let cool. Seal the jars and store in a cool place.

APPLE SAUCE

6.6 lbs (3 kg) apples
2.2 lbs (1 kg) sugar
2 cups (500 ml) water
zest and juice of 1 lemon
a pinch (1 g) ascorbic acid

Make a simple syrup by boiling sugar and water.

Peel and core the apples, cut them into wedges and put them in the syrup.

Put the saucepan on the stove and cook slowly to a mush, while stirring. While cooking, add the grated zest and lemon juice. When the sauce is smooth, add the ascorbic acid.

Pour the sauce into well-cleaned glass jars while it's still warm and leave to cool. Store in a cool place.

STRAWBERRY *In 1714 farmers crossed the Chilean pineapple wild strawberry with the North American "scarlet wild strawberry". This new fruit was used to create a hybrid with the wild strawberry that grows in Sweden, the musk strawberry. At the end of the 1700s they succeeded in creating a large, sweet wild strawberry, which is today's common strawberry.*

ROWAN JELLY

Rinse berries and apples and cut the apples into wedges with the peel and cores still on.

Cook the apples and berries for 20 minutes with the water, strain and measure the juice. For each liter of sour juice, use 3.5 cups (900 ml) sugar.

Cook it all on low heat while stirring for 10–15 minutes or until the syrup passes the jelly test: try using a spoon, if the drops fall off heavy or slowly the jelly is finished. Let it cook for another 5 minutes and skim off the foam if necessary.

Pour the jelly into warm glass jars, fill them to the rim as jelly reduces in volume. Allow the jelly to sit till the next day with the lid open. Seal the jars and store them in a cool place.

2.2 lbs (1 kg) European rowanberries
a heaping pound (500 g) tart apples
4 cups (1000 ml) water
3½ cups (900 ml) sugar per 4 cups (1 liter) syrup

154. Red currant jelly

RED CURRANT JELLY

Cook wine and berries with sugar, and skim off carefully. When sugar has melted, mix it all with an immersion blender and strain through a fine sieve.

Whisk the agar agar in to the strained liquid and let it come to a boil, then lower the heat and continue cooking while whisking for two minutes.

Pour the liquid in to a bowl or jar. Let it solidify in the refrigerator.

You can either serve the jelly as it is in the bowl, cut it into pieces, or break it up with a balloon whisk. Serve the jelly with meat dishes. The berries can be replaced by practically any kind of berries.

1.3 lbs (600 g) very ripe red currants
1 scant cup (200 ml) wine
7 oz (200 g) sugar
2 tablepsoons (10 g) agar agar powder (a vegetarian gelatin substitute available in well-stocked grocery stores)

PICKLED BEETS

2.2 lbs (1 kg) red beets
salt
water

BRINE
½ cup (100 ml) vinegar
1 scant cup (200 ml) sugar
1½ cups (300 ml) water
1 cinnamon stick
2 cloves
bay leaf
1 star anise
4 black peppercorns

Wash the beets and put them in a large pot. Cover them with water and salt.

Boil them until they are soft and release easily from a small paring knife.

Meanwhile boil the water for the brine and add the sugar, spices and vinegar. Let sit for a while by the side off the stove.

Peel the beets by hand, and use gloves if you like; it makes them last longer and you won't get red fingers.

Place the beets into sterilized jars and fill them with warm brine. Decide whether you want the spices or not, otherwise strain to remove them first. I like to keep them in, that way you can get a jar out and cut the beets in any size and shape just before serving.

Let the beets and brine cool in the jar, seal them, and keep cool. Make sure to use very clean utensils when taking beets out of the jar, and store the jar in the refrigerator after it's been opened.

PICKLED CUCUMBERS

Clean and wash the cucumbers thoroughly. Place them together with half the salt in a bowl and let sit cold overnight.

After that wipe off the liquid formed by the salt. Boil the water for the brine. Add vinegar, spices, the remaining salt, and sugar.

Place the cucumbers with mustard seeds and the dill in sterilized jars, preferably dried in the oven at 212°F (100°C) for about 5 minutes.

Pour the brine over the cucumbers and let cool uncovered, then seal and store the jars cold. Store the jars in the refrigerator after it's been opened.

2.2 lbs (1 kg) fresh cucumbers

BRINE
4 cups (1000 ml) water
*1 scant cup (200 ml) vinegar
  (12% acidity)*
½ cup (100 ml) salt
2 teaspoons sugar
5 seeded tops of dill
1 tablespoon mustard seeds

157. Quick pickled cucumbers

QUICK PICKLED CUCUMBERS

Make the brine by cooking vinegar, sugar, and water. Wash and slice cucumbers thinly and salt them lightly.

Let them sit at room temperature for one hour, and then squeeze out the water of the cucumbers.

Pour the cold brine over the cucumbers and put something heavy on top to press down. Leave for at least 6 hours before serving them, and just before you do, pour off the liquid and toss the cucumber with the chopped dill.

3 cucumbers
salt

chopped dill

BRINE
¼ cup (50 ml) vinegar
½ cup (100 ml) sugar
¾ cup (150 ml) water

PICKLES

1 head cauliflower
3 orange carrots
3 yellow carrots
7 oz (200 g) yellow garden
onions
salt

BRINE
¼ cup (50 ml) distilled white
vinegar (24% acidity)
2 tablespoons white wine
vinegar
½ cup (100 ml) sugar
¾ cup (150 ml) water
1 tablespoon mustard seeds

Make a brine of distilled white vinegar, white wine vinegar, sugar, water, and mustard seeds.

Peel, clean, and cut vegetables into small pieces, the cauliflower into florets, carrots into cubes or triangles. The onions can be kept as is they are if they are small.

Bring a large pot of water to a rolling boil and salt generously. Put the cauliflower in a wide fine mesh strainer that fits in the pan and immerse in the water on high for 2 minutes.

Then lift them up, rinse them quickly in cold water, and place them in a clean glass jar or other container.

Repeat with yellow carrots, onions, and orange carrots, in that order.

Pour the hot brine over the vegetables and let cool. Seal the jar and then store in a cool place. Store the jar in the refrigerator after it's been opened.

PICKLED QUINCE

Wash apples thoroughly and cut them in half. Put them in a robust freezer bag.

Make a light caramel of the sugar and a little bit of the water. Scrub the lemon and peel long strips with a potato peeler.

Add the remaining water and vinegar to the caramel and let it cool enough so that it can be poured into the plastic bag.

Add lemon zest, squeeze the bag so that as little air as possible is left and close it. Allow the apples to stay at least six hours in the bag before serving.

You can then add apples with the sugar and vinegar brine to a glass jar or other container which is well cleaned and dried in the oven at 212°F (100°C) for about 5 minutes. Store the jar in cold place.

2.2 lbs (1 kg) quince

BRINE
¼ cup (50 ml) sugar
¼ cup (50 ml) water
2 tablespoons white wine
  vinegar
zest of 1 lemon

FLOUR, GRAIN, & EGG DISHES

Preserved eggs, hot buckwheat cereal, and major baking

Before we had our own chickens as pets, we took eggs from forest birds, gulls, and ducks. Even when we began to acquire domestic fowl, the availability of fresh eggs remained uneven throughout the year because hens only laid eggs in the spring and summer. In the 1800s, people found a solution and began to preserve their eggs, first in water and ashes and then in water mixed with sodium silicate. These were called water glass eggs. The preserved eggs could neither be boiled nor fried, but they were good to use in doughs and pancakes in order to use all the nutrients. In *Husmoderns kokbok (The Housewife's Cookbook)* there is a description of when it is best to preserve and why.

"Preserves should be made in the spring, when eggs are at their cheapest. Preserved eggs may be used successfully in cooking and baking, since the egg white is not meant to get whisked to a foam."
-Husmoderns kokbok (The Housewife's Cookbook)

Since it was expensive to heat the oven, major baking was limited to one day every three months. But we can read about exceptions in the southern parts of the country where they baked every 14 days because the high humidity gave the bread a shorter shelf life. Crisp bread is especially associated with Sweden. Besides the great taste, it had two advantages: it was more filling and it had a longer shelf life than soft bread. Crisp bread is especially associated with Sweden hung it up in the ceiling on a rod; even today there are crisp breads that still are made with a hole in the middle. Wealthier families spread butter on their sandwiches, but the more common practice was to advantage of animal fat from slaughter and render that fat to spread on sandwiches.

But people also baked soft bread. In northern Sweden, much of this bread was made with barley, while in the eastern and southern parts with rye, and in western Sweden mostly with oats. Even the soft bread was hung from the ceiling, where it was dried until it was rock hard and could only be dissolved in a hot soup. The wheat flour was the most expensive flour and was used mainly for holidays. That was the only time when people could afford to eat the bread fresh as we do today.

The main dishes and sides mainly consisted of the four types of grain (oats, barley, wheat and rye), and were created for two main reasons: they are cheap and they saturate very well. These were used to create dishes including pancakes, waffles, and all kinds of dumplings used as a toppings for soup. But the main carbohydrate source was from barley, buckwheat, and oats as hot cereal. In some families, it was a staple dish three to four times a day, and if there were leftovers they were saved and fried the next day. When families wanted to have a special treat the cereal would be served with a little jam.

232

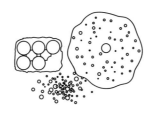

In all parts of Sweden we have dishes based on flour, salt, and water, sometimes mixed with eggs and milk, and often served with pork and something sweet and sour, such as lingonberries or apples.

Examples include egg pancake from Skåne, dumplings from Öland, dumplings of various kinds from northern Sweden, and pancakes in different forms. We also have a baking tradition, and almost every village has its own recipe for flat bread, crisp bread, or spiced syrup bread. At my Restaurang 1900, such bread is very popular.

Bread culture in Sweden and around the world is constantly changing. While I think change is great, I also think it's important to continue making our old family recipes.

As bread culture changes so do our habits, and eating carbohydrates is now seen by many as a sin. But I love bread, and nothing beats a food coma!

POTATO DUMPLINGS

2.2 lbs (1 kg) potatoes of a
mealy variety
1½ teaspoons salt
¾ cup (150 ml) barley flour
¾ cup (150 ml) rye flour
1 scant cup (200 ml) flour
7 oz (200g) salted cured thick
cut bacon

Grate the potatoes nicely and put in a colander to drain the excess liquid.

Mix potatoes with remaining ingredients for the dough and allow the dough to rest for about 1 hour in order to make firm dumplings.

Cut the bacon into small cubes and boil a large pot of salted water.

Shape the dumpling dough into balls and make a hollow in each ball and fill it with pork.

Reduce the heat slightly on the stove and cook the dumplings slowly for 35–40 minutes.

Serve the dumplings with no cook lingonberries or lingon-berry jam and butter.

PANCAKE WITH THICK-CUT BACON

Preheat the oven to 440°F (225°C).

Mix the eggs with half the milk and flour to a smooth batter and then dilute it with the remaining milk. Add salt. Fry the bacon crispy in a hot frying pan.

Line a baking tray with parchment paper and pour the batter into the pan. Sprinkle the fried bacon evenly over the batter and bake the pancake in the oven for 25–30 minutes until it is golden-brown. Serve the pancakes with lingonberries or lingonberry jam.

2½ cups (600 ml) milk
3 eggs
1 teaspoon salt
1½ cups (300 ml) flour
7 oz (200g) salt-cured thick-cut bacon

162. Egg pancake from Skåne

EGG PANCAKE FROM SKÅNE

Preheat the oven to 350°F (175°C).

Mix all the ingredients for the batter. First mix the eggs with the flour and half of the milk. Then dilute with the remaining milk and add salt and sugar.

Heat a cast iron pan with an ovensafe handle on the stove and melt a large knob of butter in it. Pour in the batter and reduce the heat. If you have smaller pans, use two. Cook the pancake on the stove until it begins to brown around the edges.

Finish baking the egg pancake in the oven for 10–15 minutes, until it turns a nice golden-brown color on top and has set itself firmly in the middle. Check with a paring knife if you need.

Slice and fry the bacon in a hot pan until it become crispy. Slice the apples into wedges and add them to the bacon. Serve with the egg pancake and drizzle syrup over everything.

8 eggs
3.5 cups (800 ml) milk
2 scant cups (450 ml) flour
2 tablespoons sugar
½ tablespoons salt
butter for frying

FOR SERVING
4 Swedish tart apples
7 oz (200 g) salt-cured thick-
   cut bacon syrup

OVEN OMELET WITH MUSHROOM STEW

OMELET
5 eggs
1 scant cup (200 ml) milk
1 scant cup (200 ml) cream
salt

MUSHROOM SAUCE
7 oz (200 g) mushrooms in
season
butter
salt and freshly ground black
pepper
2 cups (500 ml) milk
1 knob of butter
2 tablespoons flour
salt
white peppercorns
nutmeg

Preheat the oven to 350°F (175°C).

Mix eggs, milk, and cream and season with salt.

Pour the mixture in a buttered ovenproof dish and bake in the oven until it's firm in the middle. Gently shake the mold to see if it is still runny. If so continue baking for a little while.

Meanwhile, make the sauce. Heat up the milk with peppercorns and pull to the side. Melt the butter in a saucepan and whisk in the flour. Strain and pour the milk into the butter and flour while whisking constantly. Cook for about 15 minutes and whisk thoroughly, make sure it does not stick to the bottom.

Clean and cut the mushrooms with a paring knife. Fry them in a hot pan with butter and season with nutmeg, salt, and pepper.

When the omelet is done, take it out and let rest for about 5 minutes. Pour the sauce over the omelet and spread the cooked mushrooms evenly over the pan.

Serve the omelet as part of a buffet or for lunch with bread and salad.

CREAMY EGGS

This cooking method for eggs has been very popular in recent years in restaurants worldwide. These restaurants use an immersion circulator, a gadget that manages the temperature in a double boiler, but it this could also be done in an oven with a steaming function, or by using an electric kettle, a pan, and a thermometer. This requires more attention from the chef because the temperature has to be checked all the time, but it's worth it, as a creamier and tastier egg is hard to find.

Boil water in an electric kettle and pour it into a saucepan. Set the pan on the stove over low heat, place a thermometer in the saucepan and dilute with cold water until the water stays at 147°F (64°C). If you have a steaming function on your oven, set it to 100% steam, and set 147°F (64°C).

Place the room temperature eggs in the water/oven and leave them there for 1 ½ hours.

IF YOU PREPARE THEM IN A PAN: Check the temperature occasionally, and always have hot water in the boiler ready to bring up the temperature, and use cold to reduce it.

After 1 ½ hours, cool down the eggs in cold water if they are not going to be served directly. Serve the eggs in a soup, such as spinach soup.

They last for about 1 week in the refrigerator, so make a few if you like, take them out and let them reach room temperature, or heat them with their shells in some warm water for about 5 minutes.

4 room temperature organic eggs

KROPPKAKOR
(BOILED POTATO DUMPLINGS)

DOUGH

1.5 lbs (700 g) peeled potatoes
of mealy variety
¾ cup (150 ml) potato starch
3 egg yolks
3.5 tablespoons (50 g) butter
and an additional 7 tablespoons
(100 g) for serving
1 teaspoon salt

FILLING

14 oz (400 g) salt-cured thick-
cut bacon
2 pinches ground allspice
1 yellow onion

Melt 7 tablespoons (100g) butter in a saucepan and let it brown until you smell a nutty flavor and the milk proteins starts to get color. Pull it aside and let cool.

Boil potatoes in salted water until completely cooked through, leave them to steam, and then mash it with a potato ricer. Mix 3.5 tablespoons (50 g) of butter with the riced potatoes, egg yolks, salt, and potato starch. Save the rest for serving.

Chop the onion finely and dice the bacon. Fry the bacon first and then the onion in the fat. Season with allspice.

Roll out some of the dough on a clean counter surface, divide the into equal parts and roll balls out of them. Make a small hole in each ball and fill it with onions and bacon. Roll the ball again. Cook the dumplings in salted water and serve with lingonberry sauce and browned butter.

KROPPKAKOR (BOILED POTATO DUMPLINGS) The earliest record we have of someone eating *kroppkakor* is in 1775 and the man was an academic lecturer named Anders Gustaf Barchaeus. Potatoes had not reached Sweden by that time, so the dumplings were made from wheat flour. One theory is that the potato dumpling was the poor man's version of the pirogue. Later potatoes replaced the more expensive rye, which is how we know *kroppkakor* today.

165. Kroppkakor (boiled potato dumplings)

BUTTER *Butter is composed of 80 percent milk fat and 20 percent water, salt, and various substances from milk. To churn butter was originally a way to preserve the milk fat and then be able to store and eat it the rest of the year. This product was also popular at the farmer's market, and by selling butter people could get money for their household. The butter was heavily salted to keep it from going rancid, a practice that is still in use today.*

MARGARINE *Margarine was created during the wars when soldiers needed something for their bread that could keep during the trips at sea. Napoleon III gave orders to a chemist by the name of Hippolyte Mège-Mouriès to develop a product that would meet the requirements. After five years and many attempts, he managed to make a butter imitation from beef's tallow. The new product was lustrous like pearls and therefore was given the Latin name for pearl, margarine, which in Swedish became* margarin. *The first margarine factory was started in Sweden in 1881.*

COUNTERFEIT BUTTER AND MARGARINE *Counterfeit food is not only a modern phenomenon. The author Lotten Lagerstedt explins in her book* Kokbok för skolkök och enkla hem (Cookbook for Home Economics Classes and Simpler Homes) *how vendors often mixed in a lot of salt or mixed a good butter with one of lesser quality. "Well, real butter is light yellow, smooth, firm, and consistent, has a sweet taste, like that of nuts, and a fresh smell."*

Of margarine she writes "This, the so called oleomargarine, is a good and extremely durable kitchen fat, but it still lacks natural butter's peculiar smell and taste." Hagdahl shares her view and writes that purchasing inferior butter is the greatest mistake one can make in the kitchen.

WAFFLES

Plug in the waffle maker. Mix flour, salt, and water until smooth. Whip the cream until fluffy and fold it into the batter.

Add the melted butter, grease the iron with a little cold butter and fill about ¼ cup (50 ml) batter in each part of the waffle maker.

Bake for 5 minutes, and serve the waffles with jam and lightly whipped cream.

1¾ cups (400 ml) flour
1 cup (250 ml) cold water
1¾ cups (400 ml) heavy cream
1 teaspoon salt
4 tablespoons melted butter

WAFFLES On March 25 Swedes celebrate Waffle Day, but the tradition actually stems from a misunderstanding. March 25 is actually Annunciation Day, the day the Virgin Mary was told by the angel Gabriel that she was pregnant with Jesus. In Swedish this day is also known as the Day of Our Lady *(Vårfrudagen),* a word that in Swedish language dialects became *vafferdagen;* since vaffer is the old Swedish word for waffle, this holiday turned into Waffle Day.

WHIPPED FARINA

2 cups (500 ml) water
1 teaspoon salt
½ cup (100 ml) farina (cream of wheat)
1 scant cup (200 ml) any undiluted cordial

Boil water and salt and then whisk in the farina.

Cook over low heat for about 5 minutes while whisking constantly, until the cereal has become thick. Season with the syrup and serve with sugar, jam, or fresh berries.

RICE PUDDING

¾ cup (150 ml) short-grained rice
1½ cups (300 ml) water
½ teaspoon salt
3 cups (700 ml) milk
2 cinnamon sticks
1 knob of butter

Melt butter in a saucepan with a thick bottom. Measure up rice, salt, and water and add them when the butter is melted. Let cook along with the cinnamon sticks at a low temperature for 10 minutes.

Warm the milk in another saucepan, add it and continue to cook covered for 30–40 minutes. If the grains are still hard after that, pull the pan from the heat and allow to thicken without heat for 10–15 minutes.

Serve the rice with cinnamon, sugar and milk, jam, or cordial soup (see recipe page 185).

SYRUP BREAD

Mix the spices and then mix everything together in a dough mixer or by hand with a spatula, until you have a smooth mixture.

Grease two loaf pans and fill each with half of the batter (about 2.7 lbs or 1200 g).

Preheat the oven to 212°F (100°C) and leave the bread out at room temperature to rest until the oven temperature is reached.

Bake the loaves for 1 hour and then increase the heat to 285°F (140°C). Continue baking for 35 minutes and check the internal temperature, which should be 205°F (97°C).

4 cups (1 liter) buttermilk
10.5 oz (300 g) dark syrup
10.5 oz (300 g) coarse rye flour
1.5 lbs (700 g) flour
2 teaspoons (12 g) baking soda
1 tablespoon + 1 teaspoon (20 grams) baking powder
1 tablespoon (15 g) fennel seeds
1 tablespoon (15 g) aniseeds
2 teaspoons (10 g) cumin
1 tablespoon (15 g) salt

FLATBREAD

3⅔ cups (800 ml) flour
1½ cups (350 ml) finely sifted rye flour
2 cups (500 ml) milk
(50 g) butter
0.5 oz (12 g) fresh yeast
2 tablespoons dark syrup
¼ cup (50 ml) sugar
2½ tablespoons salt
½ teaspoon hartshorn (ammonium bicarbonate)
salt
5 tablespoons ground cumin

Preheat oven to 400°F (200°C) . Heat milk and butter to 98°F (37°C), and add the yeast. Stir it in and then add the remaining ingredients.

Let the dough rise for 30 minutes.

Flour a well-cleaned surface and divide the dough into about 7 oz (200 g) pieces. Roll them thin, at first with a conventional rolling pin, and then with a special crisp bread-textured rolling pin.
Let rise for another 10 minutes and then bake the flat breads for 10 minutes. If you have a pizza stone, it is perfect to use when you bake bread, both to keep the heat and to get the proper stone oven baked flavor of the breads.

CRISP BREAD

Preheat oven to 400°F (200°C).

Grind the spices and mix all ingredients in a kitchen mixer for about 10 minutes on low speed.

Take the dough, wrap it carefully and put it to rest overnight in the refrigerator. The dough can be frozen and taken out when you want to bake it, such as in summer when it's too hot and humid to store crisp bread without making it tough.

WHEN YOU ARE READY TO BAKE: Roll out dough on a floured clean bench surface, first with regular rolling pin and then with the crisp bread rolling pin. If needed spray water with a plant mister (used only for water and baking) and sprinkle on more spices and a little coarse sea salt.

Move the bread to a sheet of parchment paper, and bake for 5–7 minutes. Turn the cookie sheet halfway through if your oven heats unevenly.

1 oz (25 g) yeast
2 cups (500 ml) water, 98°F (37°C)
1½ teaspoons salt
3 tablespoons bread spices: anise, cumin, and fennel; preferably whole
1 oz (25 g) butter
5.5 cups (1300 ml) coarse rye flour

WHEN ROLLING THE BREADS
flour
bread seasonings
coarse sea salt

Index

Sources

SOUPS

http://www.nordicacademicpress.com/oois?id=54&vid=252
Matlexikonet pp 302–303.
Punsch (Matlexikonet pp 257–258 + 346)
Cream (Matlexikonet p 112)
Milk (Matlexikonet pp 313, 212–213)

SEAFOOD

Crayfish (Matlexikonet pp 178–179),
Jansson's Temptation matlexikonet p 139 http://www.nrm.
se/sv/meny/faktaomnaturen/djur/ ryggradslosadjur/kraftdjur/
signalkraftan.196.html http://www.nordicacademicpress.com/
ooisid=54&vid=252 http://www.gastronomihelsingborg .se/gh/
node/764
Interview with Håkan Jönsson, Department Head of Dept.
of Ethnology (Department of Cultural Sciences at Lund
University) 29/4–11.

MEAT

http://www.svensktkott.se/kopa/ - April 2011
Populär historia (Popular history) http://www.
nordicacademicpress.com/ oois? id = 54 & at = 252 - April
2011. http://runeberg.org/vemardet/1969/0687.html
Kokbok för skolkök och enkla hem (*Cookbook for Home Economics
and Simpler Homes*) p 253
Viscera (Matlexikonet p 137)
Meat grinder (Matlexikonet p 188)
Sausages (Matlexikonet pp 167–168)
Cabbage rolls (Matlexikonet p 182)

PRODUCE DISHES

http://www.ne.se/rotfrukter http://www.testfakta.se/livsmedel/
article15403.ece Matlexikonet: potatos p 255
Source: Interview with ethnologist Håkan. 29/4–11.
Hagdahl, p 576

CANNING

http://www.ne.se/konservering/1151242
Hagdahl
Food Science

DESSERTS

http://www.nordicacademicpress.com/oois?id=43&vid=1281
Swedish cakes and cookies, Skyhorse Publishing
Matlexikonet p 301
Coffee and cake: Matlexikonet p 147
Seven kinds of cookies: http://www.learning4sharing.nu/
sjusorterskakor-251738.html http://sv.wikipedia.org/wiki/
Sju_sorters_kakor RECIPE: http://www.dn.se/mat-dryck/
recept/grundrecept - seven kinds of cookies
E-mail interview with Leif Walling, May 17, 2011.
Strawberry (Matlexikonet p 140)
Rhubarb (Matlexikonet p 264)

EGGS, FLOUR & GRAIN DISHES

Matlexikonet p 343
Populär historia (Popular history): http://www.
nordicacademicpress.com/ o.o.i.sid=54&vid=252
Interview with Håkan Jönsson, Department Head of Dept.
of Ethnology (Department of Cultural Sciences at Lund
University) 29/4–11.
Kroppkakor (Matlexikonet pp 171–172)
Waffle (Matlexikonet p 338)
Fattigman cookies (Matlexikonet pp 159–160)
Kalvdans (Matlexikonet p 152)
Cake (Matlexikonet pp 147–148)
Coffee (Matlexikonet pp 144–146)

BUTTER AND MARGARINE

Kokbok för skolkök och enkla hem (*Cookbook for Home Economics and
Simpler Homes*) pp 63 and 64 Hagdahl p 115
Matlexikonet; butter p 299, margarine p 204